MOOSE MAGIC

All royalties from this book will be given
to the Wildlife Reserve of Western Canada.

MOOSE MAGIC

MILES SMEETON

Drawings by P. F. Wright

A TOTEM BOOK
TORONTO

First published, 1974 by Collins & Harvill Press
Toronto, Canada
This edition published 1976
by TOTEM BOOKS
a division of
Collins Publishers
100 Lesmill Road, Don Mills, Ontario

© 1974 by Miles Smeeton

*My thanks to Beryl
for all her help and prompting,
to Pat Wright for her drawings,
and to Sylvia Stacey for her typing*

Canadian Cataloguing in Publication Data

Smeeton, Miles, 1906–
Moose magic

ISBN 0-00-211631-6 pa.

1. Moose — Legends and stories.
2. Animals, Legends and stories of.   I. Title.

QL795.M8S6 1977   599'.7357   C77-001257-4

*Printed in Canada by Universal Printers Ltd.,
Winnipeg, Manitoba*

TO PETERKIN

CONTENTS

ILLUSTRATIONS

*Photographs by Bill Herriot of The Calgary Herald

1. A Birth in the Caraganas

The Old Man River flows under the highway running south from Calgary just north of Fort Macleod and fifty miles east from the Crow's Nest Pass. It comes from the Rocky Mountains, through the foothills and cattle country. By the time it reaches the road it is a wide stream with willow bushes growing on its edges and aspens on its high banks.

At the road bridge it is already in grain country, with wide farm lands stretching flatly away to the east. Even to someone who comes from a country of mountains and trees this prairie land has an attraction of its own, in the long distances and the wide arching sky above, except in winter, when it is dull and grey and dreary beyond hope. In the spring the soil, so black and level and well cultivated, is soon covered with mile after mile of young green wheat, shimmering in the sunlight and changing colour with the cloud shadow, or with the catspaws of wind that race across it as they do across the sea.

It is not moose country. Moose are browsers and twig eaters
and like woods, shelter and solitude. Here there are coyotes,
badgers, gophers and hawks, but no moose. Yet early in June
1970 a cow moose was making her way down the banks of the
Old Man River towards the road bridge. She was in search of
shelter and solitude but she was moving in the wrong direction.
She had recently shaken off her last year's calf and perhaps in
doing this had turned towards the open country. Now she
wandered slowly through the willow bushes, her big ears
flicking lazily this way and that, her almost prehensile nose
groping for high twigs, so that it appeared and disappeared in
the green foliage – like a seal's head in the sea. Presently she
lay down, hidden and resting, for the greater part of the day.
If a watcher had been close enough he might have noticed that
her long face looked particularly gaunt, and that although her
eyes were tranquil the hollows above them were pronounced.
A cattleman would have seen that she was big with calf.

All this is conjecture, but it is probable that she was up
again and browsing in the evening, wandering eastwards quite
slowly and finding security from the secrecy of the river between its high banks. If she had arrived at the road bridge by
day, the constant stream of traffic would have turned her back,
but she must have passed it at night when the bridge was
empty, either by crossing the road, or wading under one of the
long concrete arches. Then for some reason she left the security
of the river and headed steadily north across the short green
wheat.

Daylight found her and she must have felt as isolated and
exposed as an elephant would do in the desert. A mile or two
on each side of her there were farm buildings with a few trees
about them, but it is unlikely that she saw them for she relied
principally on her ears and nose to give her warning of danger.
No doubt she heard movement of some sort from the farms,

so she continued north over the level ground. Two miles ahead of her, like a distant ship on the ocean, was another farm house. No sound came from there because it was deserted, an empty grey wooden building, small and forlorn.

Just to the west of the house, extending to the country road that ran east and west to the highway seven miles away, there was a double row of Caragana trees, a hardy fast-growing shrub imported from Siberia to control the soil erosion by wind that had caused the 'Dust Bowl'. They had been planted as a hedge or windbreak to shelter the house and its garden if it ever had one, but the trees had now grown up and stretched across to each other, forming a green roofed passage for about a hundred yards. Here the moose had arrived, and she must have been much relieved to find this sanctuary, when a yellow school bus came down the road on its way to collect children for school. The driver was astonished to see a cow moose standing beside the bushes which he passed every day without interest. He saw her, alarmed by the bus, push hurriedly into the thicket.

Driving back that evening with some of the children he pointed out the bushes as he approached the house. 'Saw a moose there this morning,' he said.

'You didn't,' the children chorused.

'You betcha I did,' he said in school bus jargon.

'You're fooling,' they cried.

'I'll show you who's fooling,' he said drawing up opposite the end of the bushes. They all peered through the windows of the bus into the thicket, but could see no moose. 'Let's out, let's out,' cried the bolder spirits.

'Now wait a minute,' said the driver on his mettle, 'those things can be dangerous. Keep behind me.' They all scrambled out behind the driver as the doors opened, accompanied by a dog that had also attended school that day, and followed dutifully behind the driver, with the dog barking beside them. As they entered the thicket they saw a cow moose making off through the bushes. She had been standing beside something on the ground and as they approached more closely they saw that there were two moose calves lying close together, neither of them cleaned.

'Come on,' said the driver, 'we want to be out of this before she comes back. They can be real mean with calves.' The children, silent now, trooped quickly out of the coppice but the moose never came back. A few yards from the end of the trees she stopped and looked back, her huge bell-like ears extended towards the noise of movement at the place that she had left. Then she ran on again with her long high-stepping trot, so apt for deep snow or fallen timber but out of place in wheat. She stopped once more and listened, then moved on again more slowly towards the river from whence she had come. At close range she would have looked as moose always look. As if for ages untold she had supported all the sorrows of the world.

Next evening Peter Bergen, who owns one of the farms between which the moose had passed early on the preceding morning, was sitting in the kitchen of his house, about to have a cup of coffee after a long day's work. The youngest children, adopted twins, were in bed. One of his own and other adopted children together with sundry cats and dogs were inside and outside the house, for Mrs Bergen is an all-welcoming mother. The country was still and it was almost time for bed when a car drove into the yard with neighbouring friends from a farm.

'Did you hear about the moose calves?' asked Peter's friend over a cup of coffee. 'No,' said Peter, for his children had not gone to school by that road, but he heard the story now. 'I went to see them this morning,' the friend finished, 'but neither of them had been cleaned and the bull calf was dead already.'

'And you left the other?'

'Well I couldn't take it with me. I was on the job you see. It'll be dead now anyway. It's over ten hours since I saw it and it'll be thirty since it was born. It's no good your thinking of going. You're just wasting your time.'

'Well,' said Peter, 'I'm going anyway.'

'And why do you think the cow never came back then?' the friend asked.

Peter drained his coffee and stood up. 'Because it was too quick,' he said. 'If she had licked them dry she'd have got the feel for them and she'd have been back. They don't mean anything to her now. Maybe it's just as well or the children would have been in trouble. I can't leave it like that. I'd better be off.'

'I'll get the calf's bottle and get some milk ready,' said Mrs Bergen.

'You do that,' said Peter, 'I'll be back soon.'

He found the calf easily with the help of a flash and carried it back to the car. He took it home. It was far gone, but after warming it and rubbing it, the calf recovered sufficiently to take some warm milk from the bottle. Next morning it was on its legs and trying to follow Peter. It had become the darling of the children, but only Game Farms are allowed to keep wild animals in Alberta. Peter Bergen telephoned the Calgary Zoo.

2. The Sailors come home from the Sea

Three years before Peter Bergen discovered the moose calf still alive in the Caragana thicket, Beryl and I, with our daughter Clio, had arrived from Victoria, coming from Japan in our forty-six foot ketch *Tzu Hang*. Clio soon went off to Rhodesia, and presently returned with two rhinoceros, a buffalo and an ostrich for the Calgary Zoo, together with sundry smaller animals that she had collected herself. She managed to get them unloaded during a dock strike in Montreal and shipped them across Canada in a large truck. They all arrived in splendid condition at Calgary and Clio was forthwith given the job of running the Children's Zoo.

Meanwhile Beryl and I, down at the coast in *Tzu Hang*, had been hoping to buy a property which would provide an anchorage for *Tzu Hang* and a place where we could build a house. We did not want to occupy it immediately as we intended to sail to England to complete an east about passage round the world. Waterfront prices had risen astronomically while we had been away and we were making no progress. We decided to motor up to see Clio in Calgary.

It was raining when we left British Columbia and perhaps it was a special day when we arrived in Alberta, but as we left the mountains and the trees and saw the winding river, the bare hills, the distances and the sky so high and unsullied with bright sun above, we thought that it was a country in which we might live happily. The hay was not yet cut and the country was green, but it reminded us of a time when we were first married and lived in an equally high land in North West India, barer than this one, with mountains hemming in narrower valleys, but with the same clear sky above. Perhaps that was why we liked it so much, or perhaps it reminded us of the sea.

'Well, why not,' I said, 'we can't go on sailing forever. Sooner or later we'll have to buy some land and build a house.'

'We might look around,' said Beryl cautiously, 'but I want to see what Clio is up to. All these letters arriving from Africa in the same handwriting. I'm sure that she has something on. Anyway,' she added, 'with prices going up the way they are we might as well get something somewhere, otherwise we will never be able to afford it.'

We found Clio at the Children's Zoo. Her long legs were in the tightest of blue jeans and her hair tied behind her head in a pony tail. She was cutting up a cucumber to feed a porcupine, and a badger was lying on the cement floor just behind her in the Zoo kitchen. 'You have to look out for him,' she said, 'he looks just like a mat. It doesn't matter if you fall over him as nothing can hurt him.' In this atmosphere of animals and children, with several girls to help her, she seemed completely happy.

Later on, as we looked for a motel that would take us and the cat, and Clio and her owl, for Clio always has an owl about her, we discovered that the 'something on' was Alex

Matheson, a young geologist that she had met in Zambia.

'Oh you'll like him,' Clio said. 'He's coming out in August so that we can get married. Would that be all right? Then we are going to South Africa.'

We had a quick look round the country and bought a property about thirty miles west of Calgary and fourteen miles north west of Cochrane, on the edge of the foothills. Part of it was overgrazed grassland, and the western part was untouched, a mixture of aspen, spruce, birch scrub and grass. There was a good pond in this quarter section, covering several acres, with wild duck on it. The land here was a renewal after fire of long ago and now half-way back to spruce forest.

'Now I'll be able to keep some horses again,' I said.

'And Mummy can have a game sanctuary,' said Clio.

'What on earth do I want a game sanctuary for?' asked Beryl.

'For threatened animals,' she replied. 'Bill McKay at the Zoo has been telling me about them. Wood buffalo, musk ox, even the mountain goat is threatened. The prairie dog has gone and the black-footed ferret that preyed on it. The little northern kit fox has gone and do you know? the last litter was destroyed near Cochrane? It was quite harmless and lived on mice and gophers like the hawks, and no game, well – perhaps a grouse chicken or two, so we have too many gophers and too many badgers.'

'Are the hawks threatened?'

'I don't think that they are officially threatened, and they are protected but like the bald eagles, there are fewer and fewer every year.'

'I've always wanted to keep musk ox,' said Beryl. 'I think they'd be marvellous animals to have. I read somewhere that if they take to you they form a ring round you to protect you from strangers.'

'That might be useful sometimes,' I said. 'It might keep the Jehovah's Witnesses away.'

Clio and Alex were married and went off to South Africa while Beryl and I and the cat set sail for England, but before we left we had arranged for a barn to be built and I had bought a mare in foal and a yearling Anglo-Arabian.

The property that we had bought is on the watershed between the Red Deer River and the Bow River. If I ride north for a mile I can look down gently wooded slopes and wide fields to the north. To the south the land falls away with wooded hills on each side of a long valley to a distant panorama of mountains. To the west the whole view is filled with the sweep of the Rockies showing over tree covered foothills. To the east we cannot see much further than our own land, but it soon turns into undulating and less interesting prairie.

After getting back from our last voyage there was not much time left before the arrival of the cold weather, and as we had no house we decided to fly back to England. But before we left there were various things to be done. First we had to see if there was water available at the house site that Beryl had chosen in the middle of the western quarter. Then we had to arrange for the electric power to be brought in so that it would be available for the builders next year. We had to get hold of an architect to advise us about the house, and we had to do something about the wire that Beryl had ordered for her game sanctuary, two miles of it to go round the western quarter section, and there were yards and yards of old fence wire to be rolled up before the horses got cut on it.

We were told that the water table was generally at about a hundred feet and that though we were almost sure to find water if we drilled, there was an old man called Scotty Elder, who lived only a few miles down Horse Creek Road, who was a good dowser. Scotty was over ninety and lived in a little shack that was as dark as a root house. He was as straight and narrow-hipped as a young man with a long shrewd face and plenty of grey hair.

'So you are the people who have bought up on the hill there,' he said to me at his door. 'Aye, I'll come and find watter for ye as I found it before, where the pond is.'

'Oh. You found that did you,' I said – there was a well and wind pump at the pond – 'then it will be easy for you to do it again.'

'It'll no' be difficult.' He rubbed his chin with his hand and looked at me slyly. 'You'll know what the fee is then?' he asked.

'A bottle of Scotch.'

'Aye. It's always the same fee.'

I arranged to pick him up next morning at ten, but when I got back to the A Frame shack in which we were camping, Beryl reminded me that the liquor store, the nearest being in Calgary, was closed and that I'd have to go in the morning to get Scotty his bottle. I went back to Scotty and told him that I'd have to pick him up at two in the afternoon, to which he agreed.

Next day at two o'clock, with a bottle of Scotch, I stopped the car at Scotty's cottage. He was not at the door, but I could see his eyes glowering inside the dark little room like an angry badger's. Presently he came out, rolling slightly and looking as aggressive as if, in spite of his age, he was about to engage in a fight.

'When a man tells me he'll be here at ten o'clock, I expect him to be here at ten o'clock,' he said.

'But Scotty,' I said, 'I came and told you that I'd have to come at two because I had to go to town to get your bottle.'

'You did, did you?' he said, his anger disappearing like a blown fuse, 'then whaur's ma hat?'

Scotty was very talkative, particularly when he met Beryl, so much so that we began to despair of ever getting him on to the job before we had to leave for dinner in Calgary. He had brought a couple of willow twigs with him and we eventually got him on the move, but the ground was rough and he was frailer than we had thought and rather unsteady. Some of his unsteadiness may have been caused by a sup that he had taken while waiting angrily for my arrival from ten until two. He kept moving off in the direction of the wind pump where he had found water before, and we had to field him and bring him back to the place where we wanted to build. We knew that there was water at the pump but we wanted a well at the house a quarter of a mile away.

Presently he tripped and fell and Beryl and I ran anxiously to help him up. 'Nay,' he said, 'just let me be. Bide a bit and let's have a wee chat. I can find watter right here if you want it. You see them watter willies?' He pointed to some at his feet and just below the house site. 'There's always watter beneath watter willies.'

That is as far as we got with him about the water, but as we sat he told us tales of long ago and how he had once driven a gang plough across our place to cut a firebreak against a prairie fire. We had heard that he was very good at training Border collies and asked him about it.

'Well, I never hit them,' he said, 'if they make a mistake I just take their heads in my hands, and I speak to them very seriously.'

During the following winter, while we were away, Scotty went into hospital. He was well looked after free of charge and at first Scotty thought that he was having the time of his life. Later he found himself in an old people's home. He had lived for years by himself with only his dogs, a proud man come wind come weather, but that finished him. Perhaps his pride was gone.

By the time that we left for England and Spain the fence round 160 acres was up. It was made of heavy galvanized iron mesh, seven feet high, on angle iron posts, and after having had a shot at putting it up ourselves we decided that it was a job for professionals. We got two young men to do it, moon-lighting in their spare time, who worked for the company that sold us the wire. They were very quick, using a power hammer to drive the posts. We also had the drawings for our house and a promise that the electricity would be in by the spring.

We were back early in April and camped again in the A Frame shack near the barn and some distance from the game sanctuary and the house site. There was a heavy fall of snow soon after we arrived, but the shack had a wood-burning iron stove which we fed with old fence posts until the chimney got so hot that it threatened to set fire to the roof. That was the only grace that the A Frame afforded. It had no light, no water, an outside privy and the roof leaked so badly when it rained that it was difficult to find a dry spot to sleep in. Fortunately long periods spent at sea in a small boat had inured us to rough living conditions and we knew that we would be out of it at the end of the summer. But before the house was started we had to put in a road and before we could put in a road the land had to dry up.

Cochrane nestles under a fine but bare hill and is closely bounded by the Bow River, but one would not describe the village as attractive. Nonetheless, within its drab exterior there beats a communal heart of gold. One can get almost anything done in Cochrane, always in a friendly way if not always on time, and also the best ice creams in Canada. We got Dave Bryant from Cochrane to put in our road.

I had thought of a narrow drive winding through trees.

Dave who looked as if he could knock down trees by just walking into them, walked down the proposed route with us.

'Well,' he said, 'I can put you in a lovely road.'

'What about the swamp?'

'No problem. We can put it right through. There'll just be a swamp on each side.'

'And how wide will it have to be?'

'It'll have to take in about fifty yards.'

There were cries of dismay from Beryl. 'But that will ruin the place. It will look like a four lane highway.'

'Do you think so?' he said, laughing. 'I've put in miles of road like this. Miles and miles through this sort of country, and do you know what I find? A good road seems to draw the trees in till it looks real pretty.'

'But you'll have to knock down some of the good spruce trees.'

'No. I think we can angle the road round them. We'll have to take out a few aspens but you have enough of those anyway.'

'But why do you want to make it so wide?'

Dave explained that he would have to build the road up and make road ditches on each side, and for this he'd need all of his fifty yards. 'It won't look wide at all,' he reassured us. He was an artist at road building, thinking of his road as something beautiful that he had constructed with its curves and views, rather than something just to carry vehicles. He had been born only a few miles away and had often 'hunted' on our land. He loved the foothills but he told us that he could not spend a night in Banff where the mountains leaned over him and made him claustrophobic. When he left, so large and yet quiet voiced, with his huge rumbling machines, the road with its still bare ditches did seem to have drawn the trees in and to have accentuated them. Nor did his bill exceed by one dime his first reasonable estimate.

When Beryl decides to do anything she goes ahead like one of Dave's bulldozers. She had decided to do something for endangered wild animals. To keep wild animals at all by law in Alberta one has to have a game park of 160 acres surrounded by a seven foot fence. Now we were able to get a game park licence. If I had suggested to Beryl that before putting up the fence we should make sure what animals we could get, she would have said that we couldn't get any without the fence. A chicken and egg argument. We had our licence but we were not ready for any animals before the house was built. One, however, was due to arrive. Not exactly what we had anticipated and we had to keep it for the time being up at the shack.

3. Petruska

When Beryl and I moved into the shack we were joined by Kochi, a sulphur coloured bitch, a dog of the Kochis, a nomad tribe from Afghanistan. Clio had found her when returning from sailing with us in Malaya. She had discovered four puppies crying under the great rock carving of Buddha at Bamian on the road to Kabul. The Kochis had just been through the pass. A bitch had whelped and then, unable to bear the call of the shuffling feet as the camels and flocks, the tall bearded men and the cloaked women moved on, she had deserted her litter. Clio took them to Kabul where she gave three puppies away and brought one to London.

From then on Kochi's life had been confined, first in a London flat, then on *Tzu Hang*, and for the last three years with friends who ran a kennel. Now at last she came into her own. The brown grasslands, the mountains, the cold winds and the space resembled in many ways the country of her ancestors.

Even the A Frame had the look of a tattered tent about it and was certainly no more comfortable. This is what she was bred for; to roam free and to protect the encampment from wolves and bears, although the wolves were replaced by coyotes and the bears were unlikely visitors. Sometimes she discovered the dried leg of a long dead calf that even the coyotes had forsaken, which she dragged back to the shack. When Jim Kerfoot, our rancher neighbour, saw this, he eyed her with suspicion.

On the night of 16 June, when Beryl and I were already in bed, Kochi, who had been busily protecting her land against the coyotes, rushed barking past the shack towards the gate by the barn. A moment later we saw the tree lit up by the head-lights of a car.

'For God's sake,' I said, 'what a time to come visiting.' We hurriedly pulled on some clothes and went out, shouting warnings about the dog and calling vainly to her to sit down, the only order that she ever obeys and usually only when you have food in your hand. It turned out to be Bill McKay, young and enthusiastic, the Director of the Calgary Zoo, and one of the rare people that Kochi welcomes. Bill was barely out of his car and the moonlight meeting with Kochi safely accomplished, before he asked Beryl if she wanted a young moose.

'A young moose,' said Beryl, whose mind had been running on musk ox and how she could persuade the government to give her some for nothing, since they could only be bought for six thousand dollars unless she mounted a helicopter expedition of her own, which would be infinitely more expensive. 'A young moose,' she repeated in a dazed way. 'Yes. I suppose so. What does it eat?'

'Well, I'll tell you what has happened,' Bill said. 'A fellow called Peter Bergen rang up from Granum to say that he had got a cow moose calf that he had found last night. What the hell a moose was doing over in that country I can't imagine. It seemed that the children found the cow just as she was calving and frightened her. She had twins but the bull calf is dead and he has the female at home. If you'll take it we'll collect it tomorrow and bring it right here. We haven't had much luck with abandoned calves. We are always getting them but they are shocked when they arrive and prone to get pneumonia. I guess we inevitably have too many bugs around the Zoo.'

'Could we keep it in the barn?'

'That should do,' said Bill. 'It will need only milk at first, and it will do better outside if you can make a place for it. It will soon start browsing and then the young aspen and willow leaves will be just right for it.'

We spent the next day in a flurry of preparations for the moose's arrival. Down Horse Creek Road lives Lin Fenton, who keeps our roads in order when he is not at work on his farm. In the summer, sitting like a baron in his castle high up in his huge machine, he keeps the gravel roads graded, and in the winter he keeps them free of snow. The worse the weather the more likely he is to be out on the road and the moment there is a lull in the wind and the snow stops drifting we may expect to see him, red-faced and warm in his high cab, gesturing with mitted hand to another black cloud and more snow to spoil his work. During the night, after bad drifting, the rumble of his snow plough can be heard. Better, the local children think, if he were not so conscientious and they might miss school more often.

In Lin's yard in summer there is always a stack of snow fencing, light palings connected by wire that he puts out at bad places to prevent snow drifts forming on the road. I borrowed a roll from him and we put it out in the aspens behind the shack, making a circular pen which was easy to move when needed elsewhere. Meanwhile Beryl got hold of a bottle and several rubber nipples, and arranged for a supply of milk.

We are lucky in having good neighbours in the adjoining properties. We don't often see them except when buying eggs or milk, or passing them on the road, but we know that if we are in need of help they can always be relied on to give it. Our nearest neighbour to the east is Sid Ball and his daughter and son-in-law, Winnie and John, who run a joint farming operation. Sid Ball came out from London soon after the First World War, which he was just young enough to miss. He and his brother arrived in Canada and worked their way across, hitting the west coast just as the depression broke. They must have experienced desperately hard times but I'm sure that their cockney humour never left them. They came back to Alberta where Sid now farms his own land. He has a gay courageous look about him, with his ski cap perched on the side of his head and his teeth on the wash stand whatever the event. When we had a heavy snowfall in April he said to me 'What shall we do with the country now? Give it back to the Indians?' It was his stock bad weather remark. I felt that he was looking forward to a really cold winter to see how we could take it.

His daughter Winnie is a fair girl with reddish hair and widely spaced eyes over high cheek bones. Everything thrives under her care, lambs, chickens, children, dogs, cats and birds, but particularly vegetables and flowers, for she has green fingers. She gives the impression of wanting to burst out from the restrictions inevitably imposed by household cares and farm chores. The news of a moose calf in need of four quarts of cow's milk a day made her eyes sparkle.

'You must have it warm from the cow,' she said, and as she handed over the bottles twice on each following day some of her vitality seemed to have reached the milk.

At six-thirty next evening Bill McKay arrived in the Zoo's zebra-striped truck, his wife in the front seat and his daughter in the back. The little moose that had never known its mother was resting its head on her lap.

We had made a pen in the barn. I picked her up and carried her in. It was like carrying four legs with a head attached and she tended to slide through my arms as if she were liquid. She was light fawn in colour, quite different from the dark brown or black of a grown moose, nor did she have any spots as so many fawns have. The hair was soft and short and her nose was short also, not at all as it was going to be in a year's time. Her eyes were not exceptionally large but they had long sparse lashes. One eye was running and looked sore but otherwise she was in good shape. Since her first meal had been from Peter Bergen's bottle there was no difficulty in getting her to feed. Beryl had milk ready for her and she celebrated her arrival by drinking one and a half wine bottles of warm milk. She then collapsed on the barn floor and we left her to rest.

Bill and his family walked up to the shack with us. 'You'll have to watch out for the first few days,' he told us, 'I don't know what it is with young moose, but they get sick so easily and then they just pack it in. They don't seem to try and live.' As he walked and talked his eyes and ears were alert for any small sound or movement. Bill's conversation in the country is interjected with small asides such as 'Western meadowlark – not a lark but it has a pretty song.' Or 'Song sparrow – peep peep peep.' Tonight he heard a great horned owl.

After he and his family had gone I started the small motor that gave us light from two hanging bulbs in the shack. From a distance it had the slightly nostalgic sound of a charging engine that reminded me of many desert leaguers, but one had to go to the barn to get this impression. At the shack it thumped away destroying the peace of the night. We disliked using it and went to bed and got up early so that it was only in use for a short time.

'I'm going to keep a diary,' said Beryl, 'it must be unique to have a calf like this and watch it grow in more or less wild conditions.'

'It's a pity moose are not threatened animals.'

'Well this one was anyway,' she said.

'Lots of coyotes calling. I expect Kochi will keep them away.'

'Oh I don't think that they will come into the barn. Not into the pen anyway, when Kochi is around. I don't think that we should shut the doors because I want her to be brought up as naturally as possible, and she should certainly be out all day. I'd leave her out at night too if it weren't for the coyotes.'

We took the flash and went down to feed her. She was still sitting down but got to her feet and made a strange little mewing sound, like a lamb's bleat with the mouth shut. We found that she always did this when hungry. She took another bottle and three quarters. We then went to bed leaving her for Kochi to guard with the barn door open. Kochi had been introduced and had sniffed her all over, alert and suspicious. Unlike Beryl there was no question of love at first sight as far as Kochi was concerned, but then she was supposed to protect domestic animals and not wild ones from marauders. That was the whole reason of her being; but we felt sure that she would do her duty, even if she found it unpleasant.

On the second day when Beryl went to get the milk, Sid Ball met her.

'Well, how's that moose of yours doing?' he asked.

'She seems all right. She's very keen on her bottle.'

'I think you're feeding her wrong,' said Sid, the peak of his cap sticking up over his quizzical face. 'I reckon moose milk is strong stuff. If you fill her up with all that weak cow's milk she'll get a great swollen belly. Give her some Alfa with it like I do orphan lambs.'

Alfa is the local brand of canned milk. 'How much do you give them?' Beryl asked.

'Well I give them a quarter Alfa to one of cow, but moose may be different. I never raised one.'

From then on the moose was given a quarter of Alfa to one of cow's milk, but it was soon increased as she seemed to do well on the rich brew.

It was full summer, the aspen all in shivering leaf and the grass covered with wild flowers. It is a lovely but all too short time of the year. In the aspens behind the shack there were occasional wood lilies and paintbrushes and in the grass the blues and yellows of locoweed and vetches. It was a marvellous sight to see the little moose resting amongst the flowers in the shade of the aspens, the shadows of the leaves dancing about her. Through the grey-green trunks the distant mountains beckoned, telling her perhaps that this was moose country and that she was not alone. By day, unless we were away, she was quite free, but she never strayed far. She did not like being confined in her snow fence pen and ran up and down making her mewing noise. We decided that she must have a name and called her Petruska after Peter Bergen who had found her.

Beryl and I were working in the half section one day when I heard the noise of cattle and looking up saw a mob of cows and calves moving over the slope of the hill behind me. There was one rider with them and as they came down towards us I saw that it was Hugh Bennet to whom we had leased the land for grazing. He was walking his piebald horse behind them and a little to a flank, the cattle all close together, fifty Hereford cows and their calves and two bulls. As soon as the cows saw the water in the pond they hurried towards it. Hugh rode over to us, riding like a man that has spent half his life in the saddle. 'Thought I'd just ride them to the water,' he said, 'then they'll settle down.'

'But how did you get them here? By yourself?' I asked.

'We turned them out of a cattle liner by the gate on the road and I put them through. I brought the horse in the trailer behind the car.' Hugh always referred to his horse as 'the horse' and to his son as 'the boy'.

'Come up to the shack and have a cup of tea,' said Beryl, 'we have a moose calf to show you.'

'I'll just put the horse in the trailer,' he said, 'and then I'll come round.'

When he saw Petruska he shook his head. 'You'll never raise that one,' he said.

'Why not?' Beryl asked.

'When you've been around cattle for a while,' he said, 'you get to know whether a weak calf is likely to make it or not. Now I don't think you'll raise that one.'

Clio arrived on a charter flight from Spain for three weeks to see us and no doubt to see how the sanctuary which she had instigated was progressing. After a day or two she took the Volkswagen camper down to Calgary to see Bill McKay. When she got back she was obviously excited. 'Guess what I've got!'

'Not an owl?' said Beryl, almost as a matter of form.

She had indeed brought two great horned owls back as the Zoo had too many. 'They can be released,' she explained, 'when they can look after themselves.' They were both large owls with prominent ear tufts and darkish brown with a barred breast. Clio had soon fitted them with leashes and by day they sat on a perch in front of the shack solemnly turning their heads together towards whatever caught their interest. She called them Ba and Athena. At times Petruska came up to them and sniffed noses. The owls did not appear to be alarmed. At night they went into the barn. The owls were fed on mice which we were able to get frozen from the Zoo, on gophers which Jim Kerfoot's younger sons, Hamish and Quentin, shot for them, and on an occasional magpie, of which there are altogether too many.

A day or two later Bill McKay arrived with another small owl in a shoe box, a Richardson's owl; a very small and solemn brown owl with white spots on his forehead. He had every reason to be solemn for the down and small feathers round his beak and the upper parts of his legs and parts of his abdomen were missing. Wherever the skin showed it was a reddish purple as if he had been dipped in very hot water. He was not at all well and Bill thought that he must have been sitting in a bush beside the road where the municipal weed sprayer went past and that he had got himself well covered in weed killer. As is usual with sick animals brought to Clio he survived. To begin with he had to be forcibly fed as were Ba and Athena. To do this Clio held their upper mandible, bent their head back and shoved the food well down their throat. The owls looked like a patient at the dentist having a wisdom tooth extracted without an anaesthetic and very soon took to eating without assistance. The newcomer was called Grock because of his clownish face.

While Clio was with us we took him down to dinner with Bill and Lorraine Milne. We had been wished on Bill by a friend in England, and soon after our arrival in the shack, before we had shaken off our boat habits, Beryl rang them up.

'Come to dinner,' said Lorraine.

'And may we come early and have a bath?' asked Beryl.

'Of course,' said Lorraine without a trace of surprise or hesitation.

It was Bill, the architect, who with gentle hands, with understanding and wit, and from the olympic heights of his profession, guided us through the maze of pitfalls that threaten anyone who wants to build a house, particularly anyone as unsophisticated in these matters or possibly eccentric as ourselves. Both he and Lorraine radiated enthusiasm for the country, the climate, and for life in general. They always seemed keen that we should appreciate what Alberta has to offer, and during the years that we have been here it has been their habit to arrive from time to time, sunburnt and fit from the mountains or from sailing on Ghost Lake, to check up on what we are doing.

Grock sat on a curtain pole looking like a small graven owl. Lorraine, who loves all birds and animals and whom Kochi recognizes as one of her very rare and very special persons, was worried that he had nothing to eat while we were doing ourselves so well at the table. 'Give him a piece of paper,' Clio suggested, 'and he will be quite happy.' This she did and he tore up little bits of paper while we ate, and dropped them to the floor.

Grock recovered. He was a solemn little owl who liked to live indoors where he was always free, but one day, without saying goodbye, he flew away. Ba and Athena were also released. Athena stayed around until the winter when perhaps she went south in search of food but Ba, I believe, came to a sad end. I found an owl dead on the road about four miles away. She was in good condition but I suppose had been on the road when a car came and blinded her with its headlights. Of course one horned owl looks much like another, but this one wasn't Athena, who was larger, and it looked like Ba.

A few days after the cattle had arrived a cow and a calf found their way into the aspens where Petruska was lying. She appeared interested and, although she did not go up to the cow, who paid no attention to her, she approached to within fairly close range. Later a throng of cattle came up to the barn and advanced curiously towards her. This put Petruska into her first panic – she had to be rescued and the cows driven away.

By this time Beryl was taking her for regular walks and generally behaving as she thought a moose mother would do. A moose might not have been surprised at Beryl's behaviour but anyone else would have been astonished, for she wandered about herself, browsing off aspen leaves and willow shoots and occasionally calling, 'Petruska, Petruska. Look Petruska.' Petruska was smaller than Kochi and quite hard to see anyway, so it was just as well that we did not have passers-by.

Kochi used to go on these walks and as Petruska got stronger she tried to play with her. Kochi regarded all these advances with deep suspicion. She is an unforthcoming dog with all the nomad traits very strongly pronounced. To be singled out for any special display of affection is an extraordinary compliment. She shows tribal rather than personal affection, allegiance to a tent or the family rather than to anyone in particular. She regarded the arrival of this stranger with deep disgust. On walks she would put up with Petruska's advances but if Petruska came near the shack without being invited, Kochi sounded a warning, sometimes on a rather hysterical note. Once there was the sound of a scuffle and by the time that we had got outside Petruska was looking startled and Kochi was rearranging herself, with some telltale light brown hairs in the corner of her mouth.

Petruska was apt to get over-excited if anything disturbed the routine of her life. Simple things, like the changing of the position of her snow fence pen, even though there was no one else there and she was not inside it, made her wildly excited and she would dash about until she was panting with her tongue hanging out, and quite exhausted. She reminded us of our Siamese cat who when she was young used to suffer blackouts if she was frightened. The only way to soothe Petruska was to stop whatever we were doing that had upset her and to talk to her until she calmed down. Strong wind or thunder she found most exciting. At first it was pure excitement and she'd run about and strike at bushes with both fore and hind feet, but the border of panic was always near and suddenly her excitement would spill over and turn to fear. She had no precedent and there was no other moose to follow.

Her worst experience was when she met my two grey Anglo-Arabians. One was now a five-year-old and the other, the foal that had been born while we sailed to England, was now a three year old. They came up to her, ears cocked and nostrils dilating. It was too much for Petruska who turned and fled. The two horses cantered close in on each side of her as she ran, so that it looked like the picture by Lady Butler, 'Scotland Forever', of the Greys and Highlanders at Waterloo.

'Oh stop your bloody horses,' Beryl cried in an agony of apprehension, but I could no more stop them than jump to the moon. Beryl has always had the walk of a mountaineer, as straight as a lance, as lithe as a deer, but her run is something else. Her toes are inclined to turn out and she bends forward in an urgent desire to go faster than her legs will carry her. Now, although her will is stronger than ever, her legs are less conforming and the end result is usually a tumble. Fortunately the little brown figure, so closely hemmed in and pursued, turned and raced back at a surprising speed for one so young, and cast itself at Beryl's feet. The horses were banished to the game sanctuary.

Petruska was now just over two weeks old, and, perhaps following Beryl's example, but more likely because it just came naturally, she started to browse on the young aspen and willow leaves, which grew wherever she wandered. At first she mouthed them in an indeterminate way, but in a day or two she was eating properly and then sitting down in the shade to chew the cud. She looked comfortable and happy, her eyes placid, her big ears turning towards distant sounds, or flicking away from a fly. A grown moose has a long narrow nose and down-turned corners to the mouth which give it a lugubrious look but a moose calf can look as innocent and playful as any young animal.

'I don't know what this moose thinks she is,' said Beryl one day.

'Probably a Smeeton,' I suggested.

'And it will grow up like one too, with long awkward legs and a huge nose.'

'My legs were never awkward,' I protested indignantly.

'Once they weren't,' she said kindly, 'but I wish we could get another moose so that this one does not get completely imprinted on me.'

Petruska was at her liveliest in the early morning and in the evening. Then she drank all her milk and asked for more and afterwards Beryl would take her for a long slow walk. Clio and I had gone down to the coast and Petruska was three weeks old. Beryl took her for her morning walk while the dew was fresh on the grass and the early sun was lighting the mountains to the west. The busy sparrows, flitting about the birch and willow scrub and so difficult to identify, seemed to escort the little moose as it wandered behind Beryl. On this morning it appeared listless and forlorn. From the valley behind the aspen groves came the bawling of a cow that had mislaid its calf. A western meadowlark, a yellow-chested, black-collared bird about the size of a starling, sat on a fence post and emptied his bag of silver across the country, his liquid notes easily identifiable in this rather songless land. Presently she found

that the calf was no longer with her, and when she turned back
she saw it crying and unwilling to go on. After it had rested
they went slowly back to the barn.

That evening Beryl found a small pustule in Petruska's nose.
She was very lethargic and seemed to feel the heat more than
usual, so that Beryl began to suspect that the calf was sick and
sent a message to Bill McKay at the Zoo. The Zoo veterinarian
came out next morning and diagnosed the sickness as pneumonia. He gave her an injection and left some antibiotics with
Beryl, telling her that the next day would be critical, but when
it came the calf already seemed stronger, although she panted
a lot. She did not want to be alone and Beryl spent much of the
time sitting with her in the barn. On the following day she was
still far from well and took her milk lying down with much
eye rolling and belching. Beryl sat with her all that morning,
for most of the time with her back to the door post, reading.
About midday the little calf got to its feet, staggered across
the barn floor on wobbly legs, and gave Beryl a playful butt,
as if to say, 'Come on. Let's get out of here.'

This was the first sign of recovery but it took several days
and another injection before she was completely well. Beryl
had left her one evening and had walked down to the farm with
Kochi to fetch her milk. When she got back Petruska was
gone. She already knew her name, although she would have
come to any name that we called, but on this occasion Beryl
called and called and there was no answering bleat and no small
figure came doubtfully out of the bushes, licking its lips in
anticipation of a drink.

Beryl had become very fond of this strange little foundling,
and no less so for having nursed it through its illness. Now she
began to imagine all kinds of disasters that might have occurred
while she was away, chiefly to do with coyotes, and she began
to reproach herself for having taken Kochi, the self-professed

scourge of coyotes, away to the farm with her. That night Beryl could not sleep because of the calf and was up several times during the night to look for it with a flashlight. Once she heard a noise in the barn and her heart jumped with relief but the light revealed only a large porcupine on a slow voyage of exploration.

At two in the morning she wandered behind the little aspen-covered knoll in front of the shack, where Petruska loved to lie, partly because she was completely hidden and partly because the height gave her a sense of security when she could look out through the bushes and watch what was going on. It was a still night, the stars showing and an owl hooting not far away. 'Petruska, Petruska,' Beryl called softly. Then she heard a noise and, turning round, saw Petruska trotting close behind, apparently quite recovered and behaving as if her disappearance had been part of a game.

She was growing fast but still looked as thin as a playing card and we wondered how she had the muscle in such a narrow frame to control her legs. She loved to run and to kick and strike at bushes in preparation for a battle one day with a moose's arch-enemy, the wolf. As she became stronger she spent more time with us and less time lying down hidden in the bushes, but when the big thunderheads circled round us and the rain poured down she still became over-excited and panicky, so that we had to guide her into the barn. It became more and more obvious that she needed a moose to tell her what was what, or at least a companion to share this strange experience of a life in which she had to discover everything herself.

By now we had had Petruska for six weeks. One morning I turned on the radio to get the news and heard the reporter say: 'There was a strange visitor in town this morning. People going early to work discovered a moose on Memorial

Drive. The police are now trying to drive it out of the city.'

'Did you hear that?' I called to Beryl who never listens to the news and yet is more aware of what is going on than most people. 'There's a moose in the town. The police are driving it out.'

'I wonder if it will do for Petruska,' she said, 'I'll ring them up.'

'No, Madam,' they replied. 'We haven't caught it yet. I'm in touch with the patrol car and it's moving nicely down Memorial Drive, heading west. They hope to get it out into the country. Yes, we'll let you know if we have to catch it.'

A little later the telephone bell rang. 'Can you take another moose?' a voice asked.

'Oh yes,' Beryl replied, 'have you got it for me? Is it all right?'

'It's at Wetaskiwin a hundred and forty miles away.'

'Good heavens. How did it get there? Aren't you the Calgary police?'

'This is Peter from the Zoo. A Fish and Wild Life Officer has it at his house. It was caught up in fence wire and deserted. A young bull calf. If you can take it we'll collect it and bring it straight to you.'

'Of course,' said Beryl, delighted. We heard no more from the police and presumably they herded their moose off into the country again, which he had left so unwisely. He had probably come down the river bank at night and found himself in town in the morning.

4. The Coming of Peterkin

The moose calf arrived on 3 August in the Zoo truck. He looked in bad shape. His coat was staring and off in patches, his legs and face scarred with wire and his eyes bloodshot. He had a wondering look, and as he was brought into the barn he reminded me of a lonely child being led unwillingly to a party.

Petruska was delighted to see him and recognized him immediately as one of her own kind. She ran up to him gaily and soon gave him such a hearty butt that he nearly fell down. Beryl tried him with the bottle but he refused it. Then she tried with a bucket of milk and her finger as a farmer starts a calf drinking, but with no success.

'Well you soon haf him right now,' said Helgi, the burly and optimistic keeper from the Zoo who had brought him. He slammed the zebra-striped door and hurried off home to his supper. We cut many branches of young aspens and put them in the barn. The young moose ate ravenously for half an hour and Petruska who had never been keen on browsing ate with him as if she had been half-starved too. Soon they were resting together and Beryl left a bucket of milk in the pen.

Next morning the milk was gone and from then on the bull calf drank freely from the bucket while Petruska continued to take her ration from the bottle. We tried him on a mixture of calf milk substitute mixed with water and canned milk, but he did not do so well on it as Petruska on her diet of cow's milk and canned milk mixed, so we put them both on the same mixture until they were older. The new calf was taller than Petruska but less robust. 'What shall we call him?' asked Beryl.

'Call him Peterkin, after Peter at the Zoo who rang you up about him,' I suggested, 'it goes well with Petruska.'

On the second day after his arrival, Beryl went early to the barn to let the moose out of their pen. It was a wonderfully fresh and cool morning with the sun still low enough to cast long shadows. A sharp-tailed grouse, sitting on the tallest shoot of a young spruce tree near the barn, cackled as it flew off with short strong wing beats, before gliding out of sight behind the trees. Petruska was already up and waiting for the pen to be opened, licking her lips as she caught sight of Beryl in the entrance to the barn. Peterkin was lying down and as she opened the entrance to the pen he attempted to get up, but was unable to get his quarters off the ground. She went over to him and lifted him to his feet, but he stood there shaking and unable to move.

Very slowly she assisted him, step by step out into the sunlight and into the shade of the aspens. There he stood, looking exhausted but apparently afraid to lie down. His head was low, his eyes closing, and his body swayed as if he were falling asleep on his feet. After a time he started to kneel down but his strength forsook him and he fell onto his side. Beryl arranged him as gently as possible in a more comfortable position.

'I think he's suffering from exhaustion and a sort of delayed shock,' Beryl told me at breakfast. 'He hasn't got fever like Petruska had. He's not panting. He just seems to be completely tired out.'

We found him after breakfast still in the same position and there he spent most of the day with his face covered in flies which seemed to anticipate his early death, and gave us no confidence in his future. Petruska, browsing nearby, or chewing the cud in the shade of the trees, had hardly a fly to bother her. Beryl sat beside him whisking the flies away, and something of her compassion or her proximity gave him strength. By midday she was able to persuade him to his feet so that he could drink some milk from the bucket and in the evening he drank again and ate some bread. It was the first time that he had eaten bread, for which Petruska already had a gluttonous passion; she could eat half a loaf at a sitting if she had the chance.

The moose stayed in the same place that night and by the following morning Peterkin was on his feet again. He was very shaky but gained strength during the day. Since he had been caught up in the wire and deserted by his mother we thought that he had stood up gallantly to all the changing circumstances of his life but that now it was all over the strain had caught up with him and he had collapsed from nervous prostration.

The scars on his hind legs from the wire he would keep for the rest of his life; luckily they were nothing more than scars. The wire had cut deeply but there was no injury to the tendons and the cuts healed cleanly.

The two moose soon settled down to their daily routine of bucket and bottle, to being free to wander and browse by day and to their snow fence pen under the aspens by night. To begin with Peterkin had looked haggard and depressed, but on his tenth day with us he made his first attempt at play with Petruska. Compared with her boisterous and effervescent spirits it was a pathetic little frolic, but from then on his gaiety increased every day. Petruska had worried us until his arrival by her habit of going down on her knees and licking dirt as if seeking to replace some deficiency in her diet. We found that Peterkin had the same habit and stopped worrying, but gave them both vitamin drops in their milk.

Hugh Bennet had been away on a holiday in Japan and came back to see us, as dapper as ever in his western boots and his western hat.

'Did you wear them in Japan?' Beryl asked him.

'I couldn't walk a yard without these boots,' he said, 'and I'd be lost without my hat. I must say I enjoyed myself but it's good to be back. I've just been down to look at the cattle and they all came bawling out of the trees to greet me as soon as they saw the truck.'

'What do you think of Petruska now?' Beryl asked.

'I wouldn't have believed it possible,' he replied. 'If we could get our calves to gain like that I should be really happy. You know, I didn't think that she was going to make it.'

By the end of August both moose had lost their reddish brown coats and had grown the proper moose coat of dark brown or black with grey legs and a light brown face and ears. Peterkin always had a more solemn and wondering look than Petruska and was broader at the brow. Seen from behind Petruska had a small triangle of light coloured hair under her ridiculously short tail whereas Peterkin had not. This is the best indication of the sex of a moose when they are moving away and the bulls have lost their horns. All else is pretty well hidden.

It was almost time to move into the house that was being built in the sanctuary. It was still far from finished but there was a bath and a stove there and we had had enough of the squalor of the shack. We intended to do much of the work of finishing off the house ourselves, but to begin with we lived in a forest of two by four joists, like birds in an aviary of separate cages, with nothing hidden and the whole surrounded by the pink insulation of the outside walls which still lacked their inner lining. Our move had to coincide with the move of the moose and for this our splendid neighbour Jim Kerfoot offered his help.

To prepare the moose for their ride in Jim's truck we made them both come in and out of the shack for bread, hoping that they'd step into the truck with the same enticement. There had been no trouble in getting Petruska into the shack, in fact the difficulty was to keep her out, but Peterkin was shyer. We made a head-collar for him and tried to teach him to lead. Moose have been led and driven in a sleigh, but our efforts with Peterkin were unsuccessful. There was a small loading ramp near the barn where we unloaded 45-gallon drums of gasoline when necessary. The moose followed well and we thought that if the truck were backed up to the ramp we should be able to hustle them in. I have no doubt that if we had persisted with the leading, we would have had no more difficulty than in teaching a foal, but it did not appear necessary.

Jim arrived with his two younger sons, Hamish and Quentin, aged thirteen and twelve. The truck was put in position, rails improvised on each side of the ramp, and aspen branches put on the floor. The two young moose followed right up to the tailgate and after a moment's hesitation Peterkin stepped in but Petruska, who dropped a leg between the ramp and the truck, pulled back. It was too late now to withdraw and she was hustled in from behind. As she went she let fly with a hind leg catching Quentin on the eye and cutting his eyebrow slightly. It was nothing to what he was going to get later, playing ice hockey, but I was worried not so much for the actual damage as for what that might have been done with the sharply pointed hoof. It is no good worrying about what might have happened and as Jim pointed out, not many twelve-year-olds can return to school with a black eye caused by a moose's kick.

The two moose were quiet in the truck and Petruska was ready for more bread on the move. A farmer passed as we were leaving by the gate on to the road. Later he met Jim and asked him, 'What were you shipping? Bulls?'

'Only a couple of moose,' Jim replied, as if this was an everyday occurrence.

We had made a pen for them just below the house. They jumped out of the truck, a good three feet to the ground, Petruska by herself, always the more daring character at this stage, and Peterkin with some assistance from behind. Both followed Beryl into the pen, but within two hours Petruska had jumped out again and since they were now in the game sanctuary we decided to let them roam. It was several months before they had explored all of it. They liked to stay within call of the house, and to accompany us if we went further afield.

The northern part of the sanctuary, behind the house, is well wooded with spruce and aspen, although in the north-east corner there is an open area of about twenty acres and a smaller area in the north-west. The road runs along the northern fence, but the moose do not often go there because they prefer the privacy of the woods. The drive gates are in the middle of the fence and the drive curves down to the house in the middle of the sanctuary, sheltered by the wood from the bitter north wind in winter. From the house the land slopes gradually to a five acre pond made by an artificial bank, where a variety of wild duck breed in summer and where we skate until the snow blankets it in winter. Here the ground is open with patches of willow and small marshy ponds which dry up during the summer, and scattered spruce trees. The open land is covered with black birch scrub and patches of grass. Over the southern fence the view is limited in the west by a tree-covered ridge where horned owls nest and where for most of the year we can hear one hooting. In the middle, looking south from the house, the grassland slopes away beyond the fence, and sometimes a coyote can be seen crossing it and stopping to call as he goes. On the east side of the southern fence the view is again limited by woodland.

Looking west from the house, in the far distance the white pyramid of Mount Aylmer, 10,375 feet, near Banff, peers directly over a smaller feature thirty miles away, called Black Rock, like the foresight and backsight of a rifle, and giving an exact position to our house on the survey map. A short distance north of Black Rock is another mountain well known to everyone in this part of the world, called the Devil's Thumb. It is the most recognizable in all the chain of mountains to the west and sticks up like a black thumb except when bad weather threatens and it is hidden behind advancing rain or snow. Between us and Black Rock, beyond the head of Grand Valley, which lies a mile to the west, most of the country is woodland and most of it Indian or Forest Reserve. Beyond Black Rock lie the mountains, valleys, rivers and lakes of the Rockies. The moose really had very little to complain of in their new surroundings.

When they arrived in the game sanctuary the aspens still had their leaves, the grass under the trees was green, and there were flowers blooming. Outside the grass was already brown, that dead brown colour which is so typical of the Alberta grass lands for much of the year, but on which cattle and horses thrive. The fields are brown from the end of August until the

snow covers them and from when the snow goes until the end
of May, but the brown is relieved by the green and later the
gold of the aspens.

For the time being all the trees were green and the grass
below alive with dancing shadows. In a few days the first
aspens on the driest land would splash their yellow message,
but the message had not yet arrived. Around the pond the
red-winged blackbirds were encouraging their drab young to
more adventurous flights, waxwings were perching on the
topmost shoots of small spruce trees, and the wild duck who
had spent their summer there, the blue- and green-winged
teal, a pair of pintail, a pair of ring-necked duck, and a pair of
bufflehead were still about, with one or two late hatches not
yet on the wing.

The builders had not finished with the house so that we had
to be up and breakfast done before they arrived. They all
enjoyed working there, partly because it was something
different, all rough beams and black iron, with a fireman's
pole to come down on from upstairs, and partly because of the
interest that the moose provided. They had all become friends
with Kochi to whom they gave a portion of their lunches.
When new hands arrived, such as roofers and shinglers, and
Kochi took a nip at them, the old hands were delighted. Sometimes we thought that Kochi might put an end to the work.
One day I heard a shingler say, 'I don't trust that bloody bitch.
They should keep her tied up.'

'Oh, you don't want to give me that crap,' said the carpenter,
who had been on the house from the start and lent us some of
his tools when he left, 'she's different. You can't tie her up.
She's an A-rab.'

The horses had seen the moose but paid them little attention,
until they discovered that the moose were being fed. Then
they were liable to appear at meal times. One Sunday morning,

when Beryl and I were later than usual since the builders were not coming, we heard a scurrying outside and looked out to see the calves fleeing again in front of the horses. Beryl rushed out in her nightdress and I followed in my pyjamas. We had got head-collars on two of the horses, when I felt as if I had been stung by a bee. At the same time the horses started whirling and snorting. Beryl was pulled off her feet and left her shoes behind, but hung on gallantly. The horses in their curiosity had followed the moose into the trees, where an army of ravenous bulldog flies, which set even cattle running, had been warming their wings in the early sun in preparation for take-off. As soon as we got out of the trees they left us. We walked the two greys, who were the troublemakers, across to the south-east corner, a little more than a quarter of a mile away, where there is a gate which leads into the half section. At least I walked. Beryl with the two-year-old filly, which was in season and was snorting with its tail straight up in the air, danced a minuet. She still had no shoes, so that they came across to the gate with the filly circling round her to the constant cry of 'Oh you bloody animal mind my feet.' It was fortunate that we could avoid taking the road where we might have met someone, as I think that we were generally considered in the neighbourhood to be odd enough already.

Peterkin's eye was still giving him trouble and Beryl was treating it. Sometimes it looked as if it were improving but usually by the next day it was as bad as ever. Presently one of Beryl's eyes became inflamed and she could not open it when she woke up in the morning. She drove into Calgary to see an eye specialist. 'I don't know how you got it,' he said, 'but you are suffering from Pink Eye, a disease prevalent in cattle.' Beryl told him about the moose. 'I should perhaps correct my diagnosis to "Moose Eye",' he said, 'and you should use more aseptic methods in treating it. You have infected yourself, and now you are probably re-infecting him.' Under the doctor's treatment and advice Beryl and Peterkin both recovered.

Within a day or two of their arrival in the sanctuary we took the moose down to the pond. Peterkin ran in as if he had already been introduced to water. He splashed into the pond then moved in bounds, his withers and back coming well above the water until he was out of his depth, when he swam as a moose should. Petruska was much more cautious and to begin with only paddled demurely on the edge. They loved the water although they would not then go down by themselves. To begin with they accompanied us almost every day, showing their excitement on the way down by kicking or striking at bushes, at themselves and sometimes at us as they ran past on the narrow path. When they got near to the pond they left us and ran on into the water where they splashed each other, standing up on their hind legs, boxed with each other and finally swam round together. They showed the same exuberance when they came out, running about like children on the edge of a swimming-bath. Later we discovered that they were nervous of the remaining horses and it was not until we put the horses in the half section and they had the place to themselves that they went down to the pond alone, and even then not very often. Neither of them ever put their heads down for weeds, perhaps because there was none of the right weed on the bottom and no lilies. Wild moose are great pond feeders and all moose have folding nostrils that they can close in order to prevent the entry of water.

Although I remember the incident with the horses as having taken place on a summer's morning, with dew on the grass and the sun warm on our faces, yet in a few weeks all the trees had turned. It is perhaps the most beautiful time of the year when the aspen woods behind the house are a blaze of yellow as if they were trying to persuade the summer not to leave them to the cruel embrace of winter, to the time when they will stand naked and drab, frozen and half-dead until the spring comes again. Towards the end of October a sudden wind in one day tore all their leaves away and their glory was gone.

This month was a busy month for everyone. There was a constant coming and going on the pond as our own wild duck took wing and others from the north came down. One day I heard an eager yelping far away, gradually growing louder, and I could imagine that I was in England and heard the hounds, but instead there came a long skein of whistling swans, their white wings bright against a dark grey sky, a hundred or more, billowing up and down like a long Tibetan prayer flag waving in the wind, or the white crest of a slowly breaking wave. They seemed to be talking to each other, recognizing places on their route and calling attention to them.

Beryl and I were busy tiling the downstairs living-room floor, a large room which was also the kitchen and the workshop, covering up the pink insulation of the walls with cedar siding and in general getting the bottom half of the house fit to live in. Up the slash through the aspens, where the power line comes in from the road, a squirrel was busy laying up a store for the winter. We often heard it scolding at Kochi as she patrolled her land.

When we walked down to the pond to feed the duck, always accompanied by the moose, fifty or more would leave. Most of these were mallard, but there were also shoveler and American widgeon. The flocks circled the pond, sometimes so far away that we thought they had gone. We always felt regret that they should choose some other place more distant than ours and perhaps infinitely more dangerous to spend the night, but more often than not the sudden creak of a duck's wing made us look back as we reached the house, and there they would be, coming home again. A temporary home only, on their way south, for as soon as the lake froze they would be gone. It always pleased me to see the big ducks starting their descent from some distance away and sometimes misjudging so that they took off and went round again, whereas the smaller ducks turned as I have seen fighters turn over an aerodrome and dropped steeply down on to the water.

Meanwhile the moose were busy growing their warm winter coats, the hairs long, stiff and hollow, the best insulation against the coming weather. I have never heard anyone say 'It's too cold for a moose,' I don't think it can be. They were also growing, and nothing puts on weight and height so quickly as a young moose in its first year. They have to. Otherwise long ago the moose would have been exterminated by the wolves, which in hard and hungry weather, turn their attention to bigger game. By the time the snow comes, the young moose is well enough grown to keep up with its mother over long distances and at a considerable pace.

One day, late in October, the first snow fell. It had not come to stay, and only threatened us briefly. I looked out of the window in the morning. Everything looked grey and still, except the thronging snowflakes, like a huge crowd hurrying, running to take their seats for some event, then suddenly still and waiting. The moose were wildly excited about this their first snow and, as they always did for any strange event, came running to tell us about it.

By now the moose had lost their baby faces, which had grown long and narrow, serious and sad. Neither Beryl nor I can ever think of a moose as ugly. To us they are beautiful, bearing the unmistakable mark of aristocracy, of long and impeccable lineage. The wapiti or American elk is not nearly so noble, the red deer nothing like so aristocratic, and even the elephant who can trace his line as far back as the moose, is a commoner compared to him. One might say that the moose is out of place on the American continent but there must be several faces in the House of Lords that might be mistaken for near relations.

On 31 October Petruska had her first brush with a porcupine. Kochi had already tackled one and got her face full of quills, including some in her tongue and the roof of her mouth. We had heard that if the ends of the quills are cut off, the quill, which is filled with air, will shrink and can then be pulled out more easily. It is also said that there is a small barb on the quill and that unless the ends are cut they will work in. After much experience I believe that they do come out more easily with the ends cut, although I have never been able to discover a barb, only a slight roughness. With Kochi we cut off the ends and pulled out all the quills. She was very hysterical about the operation and we were only able to get them out by giving her a piece of wood to bite on instead of our fingers.

A moose is a little more difficult to control. Petruska allowed us to cut off the ends of the quills at the first session. We turned the garage, which is part of the house, into a surgery for the operation so that she could not walk too far away from us, but when we started pulling them out she soon became restless. It took several visits and several loaves of bread before we got the last quill out. Beryl and I have both reached what a polite person might describe as late middle age. In doing so we have not come through unscathed. Beryl has no great strength left in her fingers and I have considerable difficulty in bending my knees and once I am on them – I regret to say not often – of getting up again.

As we also need glasses for delicate work we found ourselves rather ill equipped for getting out the quills which needed a good firm grip with a pair of pliers. Beryl can squat on her heels with the greatest of ease but was ineffectual once there with the pliers. I could not get down low enough to do the job and see clearly and once down could not get up if Petruska moved away. We found ourselves impatient at each other's inadequacies.

Soon after we had arrived in the house Petruska came into the living room which she will always do if she gets the chance. She then tried to walk out through the sliding glass doors, still in their pristine cleanliness, which were shut. Finding this strange obstruction she reared up against it, causing cries of concern from Beryl, although I am not sure whether they were for fear of Petruska breaking the new doors or of getting cut in the process.

One day when Beryl was away I was left in temporary charge of the moose. I had been outside for a short time and when I got back I found Petruska showing Peterkin round the house. In all things so far, except when in the pond, Petruska, although the younger, was the leader. Now she had discovered the bread and shaken it out of its plastic bag. Peterkin had a guilty look. Otherwise, except for their presence, I would not have known that they had been there. This is a strange characteristic of moose. They are careful and cleanly animals. Other visitors that we have had in the house uninvited and in other places, which have included most of the farmyard animals, have left monumental signs of their visit. That they have come in at all is always due to my talent for leaving doors open that should have been shut.

The moose were now four months old, with Peterkin perhaps nearly five. They had been getting four quarts of cow's milk, fourteen cups of Alfa canned milk, one cup of milk substitute and three cups of water daily between them. Now Beryl began to think of reducing their milk intake and putting them on more solid feed. She kept on giving them milk all through the winter but now they were put on calf starter and alfalfa pellets as well. After a time these were changed to 'herbivore pellets' which are specially made up for zoos. They were also fed bananas and carrots.

In November Peterkin's horns started to appear, first as mere bumps and then emerging and covered with velvet. Perhaps due to this lavish and even exotic diet they grew with an extra tine turning down, so that each antler had three tines, one downward, one forward and one upward, the main root of the antler growing outwards at right angles to his long nose. Most of this was still in the future, for the time being they were merely bumps on his brow.

November came with snow. A friend had left me with a power saw on the half section and then driven off to Cochrane with the fuel for the saw still in the truck. I walked over to the barn to get more. It was a warm sunny day, more like summer than winter, and I was wearing summer clothes; a quilted jacket being still in the truck. Half-way to the barn an icy wind struck from the north and even before I got there I thought that I was going to freeze my ears. The barn was cold, the icy wind whooping round it. Presently I decided that there was only a frozen future in staying there and, wrapping myself in every sack that I could find, I started off to walk the mile back to the house. I did not use the road but walked across country lest I should be discovered in this unusual dress. It is a harsh country and at any time between October and March it can assert itself with freezing winds and a sudden temperature drop of thirty degrees. The moose revel in the cold. Horses and cattle need shelter from the wind and if they have this seem to do well at any temperature, but a moose seems to be impervious to wind and weather.

The pond froze so that the duck left and our daily walks to feed came to an end. The only birds that we saw now were large flocks of redpoll, the ubiquitous and hardy magpie, sharp-tailed grouse, the downy and hairy woodpecker, and the busy little chickadees, who with the woodpeckers were always working at the fat we hung from the trees in front of the living-room windows. Peterkin and Petruska spent much of their time near the house when they were not browsing on frozen twigs of aspen and willow. If we went out they loved to come with us, running through the snow at their great trot, the bodies almost gliding. So little motion is transferred to it, that they looked like two small black yachts sailing a smooth white sea. Petruska always wanted to play and would pretend to butt at Beryl, who, conscious of a future at stake, would never allow the indignity. As the moose ran they scooped up mouthfuls of snow, which at the same time got into their nostrils so that they blew it out in white puffs as if they were dragon calves.

Christmas came. Anne Bate, who often came to spend Christmas with us as a child and who, like Clio, would allow no deviation from the old procedure, brought her husband Roger, her small daughter, and numerous plum puddings and mince pies, to celebrate in our new house. Sue Bailehache, an attractive and wandering physiotherapist from Jersey, joined us, so that we had friends, snow, and dark fir trees about us, to give an atmosphere of Christmas, even if we missed Clio and her family in Spain.

On Christmas Eve the moose were invited into the house. Petruska being so sophisticated and at home in the house came in to the tree, but Peterkin had to remain in the garage, from where he could see the tree by looking over the half stable door that leads into the living room. They were both fed bread and bananas and then turned out into the frosty night. They lay in the snow outside the glass doors ruminating contentedly until we went to bed. Petruska was already about fourteen hands high and beginning to look large in the living room, rather as a yacht that looks so small at sea, looks so large in a boat shed.

January and February are the worst months of the year, the coldest and the greyest. Jim Kerfoot said to me one day, 'This is the land of hope. One is always hoping that a Chinook wind will come, take the snow away and knock the temperature up forty degrees. Often it doesn't come for weeks but we always hope for it, whereas those poor bastards in Edmonton are just frozen in until the end of March.'

Sid Ball, looking as cocky as ever, drove a team of greys every morning to feed his cattle. 'I'll keep the horses while I can,' he told me, 'I like them better than tractors. They always start.' I think that he was disappointed that we were not more impressed by the weather, but provided one wears the right clothes the extreme cold and the dry climate are invigorating. Newcomers ought to have been in trouble, but in fact we were more comfortable than we had ever been, in spite of the unfinished condition of the house. 'Well what do you think of our country now?' was Sid's stock query whenever I met him.

Meanwhile the moose continued to grow at a surprising rate and the colder the weather the gayer they seemed to be.

Clio and Alex arrived from Spain with two children. She also brought a Spanish buzzard and an African eagle owl. These lived upstairs in a big room which was destined to be the upstairs living room. Beryl and I intended to be completely self-contained upstairs, so that we could retreat to our own quarters when hard pressed by guests and grandchildren, or make dramatic entrances, if required, down the firepole.

The view of course is even better from upstairs and this was well appreciated by the hawk and the owl. The hawk in particular set himself up as a guardian of the house and should the moose appear, or a strange car come down the drive, his angry trilling would echo through the house. The owl was more concerned with the dog and the Siamese cat, the same cat, Pwe, that we had had with us on our voyages in *Tzu Hang*. Should the dog come upstairs in search of my bed, the owl always gave an alarm call, an angry 'hey!' If a stranger approached too closely, like all owls, it snapped its beak. Its most common noise was a low 'who whoo', which must have great carrying power, for often in the evening and sometimes in the early morning a horned owl answered from some distance away with a 'who who whoo'. It then came to the trees behind the house so that they could carry on a conversation, each in its own language, with less strain.

If one of us greeted Aggie, as the owl was called, with a 'who whoo', she looked surprised, opened her eyes wide, raised and let fall the nictating membrane, closed one eye in a slow wink and then looked shocked at her own boldness. If our greeting was repeated several times Aggie put on a schoolmaster or schoolmistress manner – we were never sure of his or her sex – and then, as if to say 'Not like that, but like this', replied with her low and gentle 'who whoo'. We had to admit that she was much better at it than we were. Every morning the first noise that we heard from down below was Alex trumpeting as he blew his nose, to which the owl always replied.

Aggie was inclined to fly downstairs, as the house is of open plan with a semicircular staircase, the fire pole in the centre, leading to the upstairs living room, and no doors. Presently she was banished to the garage, but if the top half of the 'stable door' which opens into the living room, was left open she'd fly through the door and upstairs again. One day when the sun was shining Aggie decided to venture outside. I had just taken the car from the garage and was about to shut the door, which is an upward and downward sliding one, when Aggie flew out. Although we saw her from time to time, she was away for several days. The bad weather returned and we were sitting downstairs at dinner, when something like a sack seemed to fall from the roof on to the stones outside the glass doors. 'Aggie,' said Clio delighted and ran to open the doors. The owl flew in and was obviously glad to be back and very hungry.

On the whole, owls prefer mice to eat; we are sometimes able to get them from the university and sometimes I find one in the feed bin in the barn. If the owls had to rely on this supply they would soon starve. Beryl and I have occasionally wondered whether we ought not to raise mice in order to feed the owls that Clio always seems to have about her, and so often leaves with us. Fortunately there is a hatchery in Calgary who let us have any number of day-old chickens, when they destroy the males after sexing. We keep them in the deep freeze and they provide an adequate diet for all birds of prey.

Shortly after Aggie's return Clio and Alex went down to Victoria. She came back with another owl. An Arctic owl with a few small black spots in his otherwise snow white plumage. She had been given it by Alan Best, for a long while the Curator of the Vancouver Zoo, to whom she owed something of her understanding of animals, for she had worked there for a while the year before she was married. Alan had given her her first owl, a saw-whet owl about four inches high. It had made two trips to Africa before it finally died of old age in Spain.

The Arctic owl was also put in the garage where it preferred a lower perch than Aggie. They are birds of the tundra and the tussock, and when they come south in winter can be seen sitting on a fence post but rarely in a tree. Aggie however liked to perch in a tree. We had made a small, high perch for him or her in the garage. Fortunately we were not so bothered about sex with the Arctic owl. The males are smaller and whiter than the females and this one seemed to fit the description. He had a mongoloid look about his eyes, a definite slant, and they were a brilliant yellow.

Clio was worried about the snowy owl as his tongue looked pale and he seemed to be off colour. She thought he had 'frounce' a dread disease to people who keep raptors; a fungus on the tongue which they get from eating the head of an infected pigeon. She rang up John Campbell, a big rancher down Okotoks way, a great lover of hawks, who was then trying to breed peregrines which are badly threatened in this part of the world, owing to the illicit trade in young birds across the border.

John Campbell said that he was coming up to the Zoo, so we arranged to bring the owl for him to see. People who keep birds of prey seem to belong to a freemasonry that a mere lover of birds cannot join. They speak in a special language and have a secret understanding. John Campbell and Clio were soon in deep discussion as to the symptoms of frounce, as to whether the owl had a fungus on his tongue or whether he was underweight and his eye too dull. John gave Clio some pills but said that they were old and might not be effective. However he had a friend in British Columbia who was getting some pills unavailable in Calgary. He said he'd try to get hold of some. Next day the telephone rang for Clio who was out. It was John Campbell to say that his friend had got the pills and was sending them.

'Oh splendid,' said Beryl, 'tell him to send them C.O.D.'

'Oh no,' said a shocked voice, 'we (raptor people) don't do that sort of thing.'

'I think that I committed some sort of social blunder,' said Beryl to Clio, when she passed on the good news. The pills arrived and the owl soon had a clean pink tongue and was quite recovered.

We were learning things about falconers too. An American

who had something to do with petroleum in Calgary came to see us; he was an enthusiastic falconer. The upstairs room was then on its way to completion but there were traces on the walls below the windows of the time when it had been used as a mews for the owl and the hawk. Beryl saw our visitor looking at the window – or so she thought.

'Isn't it marvellous?' he said.

'Yes, it is lovely. As long as we see the mountains we know that it is going to be fine. But we really ought to clean it.'

'Oh don't do that. I mean the mutes. You must keep one surely,' said the falconer, pointing to the white stain on the wall below the window from the hawk's droppings.

One day when the same falconer was with us an English professor of ornithology at the university came to lunch. He was great fun, and like most professors who do a lot of lecturing, inclined at times to be a little didactic. Something was said about falconers. 'Falconers,' said the professor, 'all falconers are liars.'

'Wait a minute,' said Beryl, 'here's a falconer.'

'I can't help it,' said the Professor, 'I've said it before and I say it again. All falconers are liars.' The falconer, however, was far too well-mannered to take offence, and no offence was meant by the professor.

I saw the first bald eagle in Grand Valley on 7 March and the first golden eagle also in Grand Valley on 9 March. Although we were still having bitter weather and the country-side was deep in snow, they were on their way north. The coyotes also were very active and we heard their lovely lilting chorus by day as well as by night. Gophers began to appear on the road and I saw the first sparrows in the barn. There were soon long icicles hanging from the roof of the house.

In almost no time the first year was over. When we were sailing, seeing so many new places and new countries, we had so many experiences that the years seemed to last longer. This year had flashed by. It had not been unproductive; where there had been nothing, there was now a drive and a house, water, heat and light. All the changing processes of building and moving in, being kept busy by the arrival of the moose, all the work entailed in making the house habitable, the changing seasons – all this should have made the year seem longer than usual. It must be that remaining in one place makes time go more quickly, and that the gypsy life that we had been leading was really the secret of fuller enjoyment of the passing days. Like sipping a glass of brandy and smelling its bouquet, we had somehow made the days last longer, while we sailed.

5. Moose Marriage

Peterkin's first horns, although still in velvet, had a twenty inch spread on 27 July. They were puny little horns for a moose, but he himself was beginning to show signs of turning into a fine animal. He was over sixteen hands at the withers already, and as they walked beside me, with their slow and stately pace, a progress is the only word to describe it, they made an impressive pair. They did not always walk but sometimes came running at us as if they were going to run right over us, but always swerving away at the last moment. While the grandchildren were with us we could never let them go out by themselves.

In August, even before the velvet was off his horns, Peterkin began to become more possessive with Petruska and did not like strangers to get between them. By the end of August he had rubbed the last velvet off and for a few days his horns looked bloodstained. From then on he became argumentative, liking to contest our movement along any path. We ignored him and walked straight at him but took care to be armed. Bill McKay had once said that the only time he has known people hurt by a moose was when they had had an inadequate weapon with which to defend themselves. Beryl always carried a heavy mattock with one blade sawn off, so that it looked like a heavy, short-handled hoe, an instrument of agriculture in use in most oriental countries. With this I have seen her give Peterkin a tremendous whack between the horns with the blunt side of the mattock that left him not daunted but slightly bemused. It only occurred during the period of rut, and the confrontation, usually over the feed trough, went like this:

'Peterkin. Now don't you look nasty.' Peterkin leant over the trough with his ears back and his eyes rolling. Beryl had to go in under the horns to put the feed into the trough, but could not very well do this until his ears came forward and he put on his usual benign expression.

'Peterkin,' she'd say, 'how dare you look at me like that?' This had no effect on Peterkin who rolled his eyes as before.

'Peterkin,' she'd repeat, grasping the mattock, 'I shall hit you.'

She looked rather like David in front of Goliath. Then she'd raise the mattock and hit Peterkin between the horns. Peterkin would give a bleat, take a few steps back, and then his ears would come forward in mild surprise. It did not always happen like this. Sometimes Peterkin withdrew in front of the blow and as the mattock is heavy Beryl nearly followed it over the trough. Peterkin, who is certainly not himself at this time, looked even more puzzled and surprised.

I usually carry a stick which would be quite ineffectual if Peterkin went for me, but he was then still a young moose and had a sense of inferiority. When he contests a path we walk straight at him, ignoring him, and at the last moment he turns and gives way. The weakest part of a moose is his back end and even in the early days when Peterkin was growing his first horns he hated to have anyone walking close behind, and would whirl round and present his head. It was very difficult to drive him, but he would usually follow without any trouble.

Petruska has her bottle

Peterkin and Petruska —
their first summer in
the sanctuary

Peterkin is introduced to the films

Snowy owls

In all things Petruska at this time was the more amenable. She was not now the leader, but like Beryl, she went her own way.

During all the summer the moose had been bothered by numbers of small black flies that clustered on their quarters and down the backs of their legs, particularly just above their hocks. Here they were so irritating that small sores developed on which the flies were always thick. Beryl would not use any insecticide on them, as she was determined that these moose should be brought up in as normal a way as possible. If wild moose suffered sore hocks from flies, then these would have to put up with it. She is anyway against insecticides and herbicides, in fact against most artificial controls, but she relaxed her regimen for the moose as far as allowing them a block of salt to lick and giving them their small daily feed. Partly because in nature they would have had more room to search for what they wanted and partly so that we might keep in touch with them. As soon as the days got cooler the flies disappeared and the sores healed immediately.

Our house is heated by propane gas and from time to time a large gas truck arrives to replenish the tank where the gas is stored. We never have to telephone the gas company to ask them to refill the tank. They know, according to the weather, how much we will be using and always come long before it gets low. Although we only meet the driver of the truck during his short visits and the company director, manager, owner and driver of another truck, Claire Flavelle, even less often, we have a good relationship with the company. We arrived back one evening in July to find a bill for propane pushed under the garage door. On it was written:

'Sorry I missed you but had a most enjoyable time what with two moose here to help me unload. The bull is the most fearless of the two as he would come practically right up to me. With a place like this I don't see why you ever leave. I don't think I would.

Tally Ho,
Claire Flavelle

The bull finally did come right up to me and I rubbed his nose. He was also quite sexually inclined towards the cow, but she was having none of this.'

By the end of August Peterkin was in rut. As he stalked about with his head up, his ears back and the whites of his eyes showing, he was, at least to strangers, an intimidating sight. Since Petruska had not yet shown any signs of coming in season, Peterkin was inclined to look elsewhere. For the first time he seemed conscious of the limitations of his surroundings and spent some of the day patrolling the fence and gazing at distant cattle as if he might find something there to assuage his budding passions.

He was obviously conscious of his own territory, limited though it might be. Since strangers came in by the drive gates, he was apt to stand on guard there. One evening after friends had left the house, I took the truck to feed the horses, and found that Peterkin had pinned our visitors in their car and that they had been unable to get out to open the gates. Visitors came at their peril. Peterkin was liable to test his horns on their cars and both moose found car radio aerials irresistible. A friend from Toronto came to visit us and when I saw the moose at her car and was hurrying down to drive them away, she stopped me, saying, 'Do please let the moose bite off my aerial. They'll never believe it in Toronto.' Another woman from Toronto who came to see us said, 'I've got to tell them about this when I get back to Canada.' I do not know where she thought she was, but there is a general complaint in the west that the east thinks us far away, possibly even on another continent.

At the end of September Peterkin came round the house after Petruska making a bleating sound. It was the first sign of her approaching season. He was looking quite friendly but accidentally knocked his horn against something, immediately he put his ears back and his eyes became suffused and glassy. It is his danger signal and I don't think that then he really knows what he is doing. If anything touched his horn at this time he reacted immediately. Even the noise of a stick hitting a tree, which suggested the sound of an antler, would excite him. He had trouble with some visitors who 'know about animals' and have 'a way with them,' and touched Peterkin on his head or his horns. To him this was an invitation to a pushing match. One might just as well have a match with a tank except that the tank would not feel inflated by victory.

At the beginning of October Petruska, although only a year and four months old, was in season. Whenever she tried to come to the house Peterkin ran beside her in an effort to herd her away. We saw them several times in the distance, running side by side, covering the ground at a good pace, with Peterkin pushing her, like a polo pony 'riding off.' Sometimes she succeeded in avoiding him once: she arrived quite exhausted with Peterkin panting behind, and threw herself on the ground in front of the house. After a time, when Peterkin had recovered his wind, he came up and stood behind her bleating, but he did not molest her until she got up, when the running and driving started again. In subsequent years, when Peterkin was trying to subdue his love, the bleat changed to a grunt.

Next day we found them in front of the house, both looking rather dishevelled as they always did these days. Peterkin was gazing hopefully at the feed trough and Petruska looked in at the living-room window. Suddenly she turned and took a few steps towards Peterkin. Then she gave a quavering bellow, as if to say 'Oh you horrible great bull of a moose,' turned and fled. Peterkin who now appeared thinner and more exhausted than Petruska replied with a protesting bleat, but he could not refuse the invitation and followed gamely in pursuit.

The day after this the wild courtship appeared to be largely over and their relations were more relaxed. Petruska was still very much in season with a considerable amount of mucus about her backside. Peterkin tried to mount her several times but she always took a casual step away at the critical moment. Peterkin was continually sniffing and licking, then raising his head and curling his upper lip. He always went down on to his knees to do this when he found traces of her discharge upon the ground. Although none of us saw the complete mating, Clio, who was with us at the time, heard Peterkin grunt and looked up just in time to see him fall off Petruska on to the ground. From the way he collapsed she thought that he had made a jump at the end of the proceedings, which had been quickly concluded. Next day everything seemed to be over for Petruska, while Peterkin simmered down more slowly and while he kept his horns he was inclined to be aggressive.

Peterkin liked to horn certain trees, and strip the bark off them. I should have supposed that any tree would have done to test horns against, but he preferred the lodgepole pine, which are much scarcer with us than the spruce and the aspens. He horned selected pine trees until there was no bark left and then came to us smelling as if he had just had a pine oil shampoo. I can only assume that he liked the smell on his head.

He was not averse to testing his horns on the doors. As he did not like walking on rough stones, we made a terrace in front of the house of rough field stones. One day perhaps we may be able to finish it as a patio, but at the moment it is only a barricade against the moose. In the garage at the front there is a seven foot door, which opened by depressing a catch. The moose soon learned to open it, so we had to change the catch to one that could only be dealt with from the inside. Peterkin found that he could also open the sliding car doors at the back of the garage by heaving them up with his horns, if by good fortune a tine caught the handle. One day while I was away Beryl came back from Calgary to find that Peterkin had done just this and had shut himself in the garage. On this occasion he had not been as discreet as usual. Most of the things on the shelves had been removed or knocked down, including a battery charger that had broken. He had not opened the feed box, but the state of the floor had to be seen to be believed. It was covered with debris and the droppings of hours of self-internment. There is a clothes line in the garage and a wall furnace that blows hot air over damp clothes. Peterkin had brought down the clothes line, but he had not damaged this furnace or the other furnaces and conduits that heat the house. Beryl had been away for the night so there was no knowing how long he had been there.

One night at about two in the morning I heard a noise in the garage which is below my bedroom. I went down and found Peterkin tiptoeing about inside, looking extraordinarily rakish with a pair of stocking tights, that he had taken off the clothes line, draped over one antler.

These adventures brought us to the sad conclusion that we would have to fence off the drive, bringing the fence on each side to the two ends of the house. Children would then be able to use the whole length of the drive without danger, Peterkin could no longer guard the gates, and our friends' cars would be safe from damage. It was too late to do this now as the ground was frozen, so it would have to wait until the following summer. Meanwhile we gave Peterkin two toys to play with, hoping that he would leave our doors alone. We hung an iron pipe between trees at the back of the house. He could push it and toss it as much as he liked. After playing with it for an hour on the first day he went off with Petruska, but soon he remembered it and came back. When he saw it through the trees he gave a playful skip and ran up for another workout on the punch bag. In time he lost interest in this toy so we put a heavy stake up on wire between two trees in the front of the house. He could push this for several yards and then turn round and push it back again, but as soon as he lost his horns he gave up his toys.

During the past summer Aggie, the owl, had left the garage and was living in a spruce tree just behind the house. She hunted every night, leaving the tree in the late evening and we often saw her float away, looking twice as big as she seemed when sitting on her branch. She was still quite tame and took chickens from the hand by day while sitting on her branch, picking them up in her bill, transferring them to her foot, and then tearing them to pieces. While so occupied, she always did a happy little dance, raising first one foot and then the other several times. If we arrived late from Calgary, after she had left her tree, she would come when called. She arrived like a wraith in the gathering darkness and lit silently on the ground near Beryl, who held a dead chick up to the darkening sky.

The snowy owl had been transferred to a 30′ by 20′ wire enclosure outside, over which we had hung netting so that he could not fly out. As he was zoo-born we were not sure how he would get on if he were free. Beryl was hoping for a female and that perhaps they might breed and the young go free. Two spruce trees stood in the centre of his enclosure, but he never flew into them or used them as a ladder for his escape, but occasionally perched on the lowest branch. He preferred a log, or even the snow itself, and like the moose was impervious to the cold.

In November the moose were very gay, often playing together and running in excitement at the first snow with their crests up and striking at bushes. Peterkin still liked the company of Petruska, and once when she was chewing her cud in front of the house he prodded her up with his foreleg so that she might come away with him. Both bulls and cows, when they are excited, can erect a six inch crest from their poll right along their backs to the tail. It makes them look bulkier and more imposing.

It was the time of bonfires. The moose break down young aspens so that they can eat the topmost twigs. They can do this by reaching high up and, with a single twist of their powerful jaws, snapping off an aspen branch two inches thick at the break; indeed their usual paths are lined with broken down aspens. We try and collect these fallen but uneaten tops for burning, hoping that what remains will send out new twigs like a pollarded tree. But even without broken tops, though hardy to cold, the aspen is not a particularly sturdy or long-lived tree and every gale leaves many on the ground. If Beryl and I did nothing more than keep the woods cleaned up there would be enough work to keep us busy.

In summer a burning permit is required before lighting a bonfire, that is if the fire can be seen. In winter when the snow is on the ground we burn anyway, assuming that no permit is required. If we asked for all the permits that are needed no work would ever get done.

One day in November, there was a low freezing mist with a north wind which built up four inch needles of frost on the south side of the fence wires and made the power lines hang in heavy white ropes. Beryl and I were burning fallen branches, the grey trunks around us faded into fog, the fog blending with the snow. We were in a small white circle with only the blaze of the fire giving any colour. Suddenly two dark shapes materialized silently out of the mist. Peterkin and Petruska had come to see what we were doing. They stood about the fire with their big ears moving slowly, their faces all frost encrusted, their look gentle. Only at times, when I pulled a branch towards the fire, did Peterkin put his ears back and roll his eyes as if to tell me that it was his branch and not mine. He was much quieter now, yet he was still a powerful and not entirely predictable wild animal. We had to remember this.

Petruska had two more brushes with a porcupine and the second time she had a foreleg stuffed full of quills. We kept her in the garage with the lower half of the stable door shut. She was now sixteen hands high. After we had cut off the ends of the quills and were trying to pull them out, she decided that she had had enough and jumped through the gap in the stable door into the living room. This was a four foot six inch standing jump through a three foot by thirty inch gap, and she knocked nothing down on her arrival.

The pond had been frozen for some time and what snow had fallen had been blown away. Beryl decided that she was going to learn to skate. I had skated as a small boy at my prep school and I had once been asked to play hockey when with the Canadian Army shortly after my arrival in Canada. I did not realize then that all Canadians were born with skates and can skate almost before they can walk.

That had been more than twenty years ago. Now we were to start it all again.

Beryl was determined that she would not fall backwards and adopted a crouching forward position. From time to time she literally flew from this position on to her knees which became so bruised that she could hardly walk. Then she bought some hockey knee pads and went from strength to strength. I was determined not to fall on my knees and soon found that I could assume a horizontal position in the air before falling flat on my back. However we survived the first few days without damage and then used to skate every day until the snow stopped it.

The moose were delighted that once more we were making expeditions to the lake. They came down with us and interfered if they could while we were putting our skates on. But they would not go on to the ice, which they hated. If they sometimes came out a few feet they walked on the tips of their toes with trembling short steps. They went round the pond and tried various headlands in an attempt to get as close to us as possible. We had a feeling of great superiority as we glided past them. One day Peterkin made a determined attempt to join us but his feet shot away and he fell. To begin with we thought that he would not be able to get up again, but in the end he succeeded; with much quivering and bleating, and with palsied steps he made his nervous and complaining way to the shore.

It was our second Christmas and this time we had Clio and Alex and their children, and Anne and Roger with their child. Since Clio was home everything had to be done in the traditional way that both she and Anne remembered. Father Christmas arrived to the sound of sleigh bells and to shouts of 'Whoa there – Dasher'. Then there were heavy footsteps on the roof and a sack of presents lowered down through the hatch for still believing children, and finally the notes of a hunting horn and the sound of bells fading into the starlit night. Petruska and Peterkin came again to the party and Petruska came in to the tree. She seemed to fill the room, now that she had grown so big, and Beryl had her usual trouble with her camera.

'Oh bother the thing,' she says, 'these useless bulbs. Clio. Keep the children quiet. They'll get the moose excited. Petruska. Look this way. Oh dear. Now it's gone off and I haven't any more,' and the result, when it arrives, is a picture of something that might be Petruska's hind leg and a candle.

The New Year also had to be celebrated traditionally. 'We must see all the animals after midnight,' said Clio. 'Do you remember how we walked to see the stork at Cota Doñana, and wished it a happy New Year? We have to go to the barn and see the horses and then we have to find the moose.'

'And the owls and the peacock,' Beryl added, 'we mustn't forget them.' We had recently been given a peacock and pea-hen who lived in the barn.

Just before midnight we found the children awake so they were brought out and we all sang 'Auld Lang Syne' with Alex who is a Scot and knew all the words leading, but Roger who is the son of a clergyman making the most tuneful noise. Just as it ended we heard a tapping on the glass doors and there were Peterkin and Petruska.

They stood on the snow-covered terrace as Peterkin gently knocked the glass with his horns, which he knew brings an instantaneous reaction from inside the house. They were in a pool of light with behind them the dark trees and the snow and the strange stillness of a Canadian night. Instead of the angry shouts with which Peterkin was usually greeted when he got on to the terrace there were cries of 'The moose, the moose. How nice of them to come.' They were fed bread and banana.

This habit of Peterkin's of knocking the glass doors with his horns was both frightening and annoying as we were sure that one day he would break them. When the snow lay deep on the rough stone terrace he had no difficulty in stepping up, crossing the terrace and putting his great moose nose against the glass. Whether, when he saw no one there, he deliberately tapped at the glass, or whether his horns tapped the glass as he licked across it, it was impossible to say but in any case the result was the same. There was a rush of feet across the floor upstairs and bodies came sliding down the fireman's pole, accompanied by shouts of 'Peterkin. Stop it you bloody moose.' Then Peterkin backed off across the terrace, his face showing mild astonishment at the reaction that he had caused, his big ears forward, his eyes round and black in the lamplight. What moose could resist such a result from a small tap on a window. There was also a possibility that he objected to the way we allow Petruska, from whom there is no danger, to lick across the glass doors in immunity.

We could hedge ourselves in with electric fencing but that would spoil the view and a lot of the fun. The answer to this rare problem was to build a wall along the front of the terrace so that the total drop was about three feet. This might dissuade him from climbing up and yet would not be a positive barrier, nor would it spoil the view but might enhance the idea of a house immediately surrounded by its unplanted garden of wild grass and wild flowers, trees and wild animals.

Moose are so alert to what is going on around them that we believe they always know whether we are in the house or not, and we hope that they do not try the doors and windows when we are away. Before the upstairs living room was completed we had sometimes to move our dinner and dishes upstairs and sit on the floor of the unfinished room, in order to avoid the moose attempting to join us in the light below.

The farm to the west of our place belongs to Bert Fox, a tall and active man, who runs his ranch single-handed except for the help of his wife. Clio's children believe that he is the real Mr Fox, Beatrix Potter's Mr Fox, and if they come with us in the car to buy eggs, look with some anxiety at the window, expecting to see his whiskery mask.

'Was Mr Fox there?' they ask.

'Yes. He was washing the end of his brush in the sink and says he can't come out because it will freeze.' One can only have the delicious thrill of a real Mr Fox living in a green farm house for a very few years. The blue-green farm house is a landmark that we describe to anyone coming in search of our home. Mr Fox also had an old-fashioned barn beside the road, made of huge logs with a shake roof. On 15 January I was at Jim Kerfoot's house and about to leave late in the evening for home. A violent wind was blowing across Grand Valley with the snow drifting badly across the road.

'If you don't ring in half an hour,' said Duncan, Jim's oldest son, 'I'll come out in the four wheel drive and pick you up.'

It is one of the nice things about this country that if you are out to dinner in winter when the weather is bad, your friends will always ring up to ask if you are home safely or ask you to ring when you get back.

'I'll give Beryl a ring and tell her I'm leaving, but anyway I'll make it. Don't you bother,' I told him but I knew he would.

On the Grand Valley road conditions were far worse than I had expected and I just scraped through some big drifts. At Fox's place the heavy barn roof with several large logs attached had been lifted right off. I could not see this because I was blinded by the drifting snow. Just before the top of the hill I had to stop. In a momentary lull I tried to make the few yards to the top of the road but my wheels started spinning. I got out, dug the snow away and tried again. As quickly as I dug the snow away fresh snow took its place. In a very few minutes my half hour was going to be up. I saw the lights of a truck close behind me as I rocked the car backwards and for-

wards on the gears. Suddenly the weather door was opened
and a gust of icy wind and snow blew in followed by a large
black dog covered in snow that leaped on to the seat beside me.
A voice shouted as if in a gale at sea, 'Can I give you a hand?'

'A shove would do,' I said, for a few yards away there was
some shelter from a hedge and the top of the hill, and the truck
was very light. 'Can you manage this in yours?'

'Oh it's a big truck. He's coming on nicely. Come on,' he
said pulling the dog out, 'you're just a big softy.'

With a short push I was out of trouble and away over the
top of the hill, taking him at his word that he could manage,
for I wanted to stop Beryl coming out in the Land-Rover and
Duncan from the Kerfoot home. After a cup of coffee and a
slightly embellished account of the hazards of the journey, I
walked to the window and looked out. I could just see the
road at the top of the hill. The lights of the car showed there
dimly through driving snow. Presently they disappeared, but
for a long time I had a guilty feeling that I might have deserted
my comrade on the hill and an almost immoral hope that he
did not know who I was. Fortunately all was well as I discovered some time later that it was some other car and not his
that had stuck. This blizzard was to bring all kinds of interest
in its wake. The snow, blowing across Mr Fox's field, had
drifted immediately behind the western fence and in places
was only a foot from the top, but neither we nor Peterkin
were aware of this at the time.

We were in for a really cold January. The temperature
dropped to twenty below and on one occasion to forty below.
This was altogether too cold for Aggie. We found her in the
morning with a rim of white frost round her eyes, but the
moose had frightened her from her low perch and we could
not get hold of her. She was drugged with the cold, life only
just flickering inside her puffed out feathers, but as soon as the

sun warmed her she recovered and took a chicken off the end of a pole. One night I found traces to show that she had huddled at the back of the garage door, where she had found some benefit from the warm air within. Next morning she was there again but when I slid the door up she managed to fly away, alarmed by the sound of the door. On the following day she was back on her low branch and Beryl caught her. She was very pleased to be back on her perch in the garage. Soon she was herself again, very hungry, and 'who whoing' to show her pleasure at being inside. She stayed in the garage until warm spring weather tempted her out. Then one day she left for good. During the summer I saw a big owl from time to time which may have been her, but she never came back to the house. We hope that she went south to a warmer climate.

6. Peterkin lost

Peterkin was better with us now, but he was a continuous source of worry with strangers. Ron Mathews arrived to introduce us to cross-country skiing. We had just started off and I had already fallen like a dead tree on the way down the road to the pond when we saw Peterkin pursuing Ron's friend, Eric Laerz, round and round the car up at the house. Pursuit in fact was carried out in a stately walk with a certain amount of coughing and saliva which indicates as clearly as the eyes and ears that Peterkin is not amused.

Ron hurried back and was soon pinned by Peterkin against a tree which he could not climb since he had his skis on, and which he could not take off because he was keeping Peterkin at bay with his ski poles. By this time I was at the bottom of a small slope which I found quite impossible to climb. I soon fell and wondered how, with my stiff knees, I was ever going to get up, but Beryl who had once skied in Norway managed to get back to the house and rescue the two men. As they were both hardy mountaineers they were not upset by the moose, but unfortunately he had paid some attention to Ron's Alfa Romeo.

'Nothing more than I'd get in a parking lot,' he said, but I felt that he would rather have been horned himself than have his car scratched. The fencing of the drive now became inevitable, but meanwhile we wondered what other damage Peterkin might do.

On the morning of 1 February I went to feed the horses. The night had been so cold that I wanted to get some good food into them early in the day. The sun was not yet over the horizon, the snow was deep with a crust that would not support a man and I could feel the cold inside my nostrils. The horses were already outside the barn and came trotting to the gate as I opened it, then they galloped beside me as I drove the truck to the barn. Inside, the peacock and peahen were sitting on the hay. Her comb had frozen and fallen over to one side. When I got back to the house I passed Petruska but there was no sign of Peterkin. I told Beryl and she called him but he did not come for his bread.

At this time they were always together so we became worried. I drove back to the gate and found moose tracks outside, evidently Peterkin had been up and down the fence several times. I went along towards Bert Fox's place and saw the moose standing outside the game sanctuary fence, in the field. I collected Beryl and we set off to get him back. He did not follow as well as usual and objected very much to being driven. We had to get him in through the drive gates, but although anxious to get back to home and breakfast, he wanted to return by the way he had come. He had stepped off the big snow drift, over the top of the fence and into some bushes that lined the fence on Bert Fox's side where the snow was lower – for some reason he did not like to tackle the small jump from the bushes. Eventually we got him through the gates.

'We'll have to get a bulldozer and take the snow away from the fence,' I said to Beryl, 'so that he can't do that again.'

'Well, you can get a bulldozer, but you know what that is going to cost. I bet it will cost three hundred dollars. Perhaps we could dig a trench,' she suggested, 'the snow has only drifted for about a hundred yards.'

We went up armed with shovels and started to dig. The drift was about six feet deep but we thought that a three foot by three foot trench would discourage Peterkin from stepping over the wire. 'I'm sure that he just did it without thinking,' said Beryl.

We found that we had given ourselves a considerable task to dig even a short trench let alone one a hundred yards long. Presently Peterkin, rested from his night's adventure, came in his companionable way to watch us at work. As Beryl and I laboured, sinking gradually lower into the hard snow, Peterkin stood over us. 'We must look exactly like two prisoners digging their grave, with a guard standing over us,' I said to Beryl. The corner of the fence by the road was fifty yards away. A lorry loaded with hay came along, stopped and backed up to the line of the fence. The driver and his companion watched us silently from the cab of the truck for ten minutes before they drove off. We dug deeper under Peterkin's overseeing eye.

When one starts on a job like this with Beryl there is no stopping. For her, because she does not give up anything that she has undertaken, and for her companion, because of a sense of shame at having to give in first. Years of life with her have taught me how to avoid these situations, but this time I had been caught out. I began to think that we might really be digging our graves, but Peterkin came to the rescue. Avoiding the little trench that we had so far hewn he stepped easily over the fence and started to browse on some willows; obviously he had remembered them from the previous night.

'The bloody moose,' I said, yet in a way I was relieved that our digging must come to the end for the time being.

'We'd better get him back,' said Beryl.

'Wait a minute. I'll get your gun and pepper him from some way away. Perhaps that will teach him not to come over the fence, and anyway it may make him suspicious of hunters. Also he may jump back,' I added hopefully.

'Are you sure that you won't hurt him? Might you get his eyes?'

'No. Of course not. I'll shoot him in the backside.'

'Oh,' said Beryl, thinking of another painful possibility.

'It will only sting him,' I assured her.

I fetched Beryl's little gun, a twenty-eight bore. Mine I considered too potent. The cartridges were Eley Grand Prix and thirty years old. I drove the car to Grand Valley road and then stalked Peterkin from the west so that he would think me a stranger. At about a hundred yards I fired at him, when he was conveniently turned towards the game sanctuary. The cartridge fired all right in spite of its age and Peterkin wheeled round and ran towards me, then as he caught sight of me settled down to browsing again. My plan was the biggest flop ever and I was not prepared to try again. For the second time we walked Peterkin to the drive gates and let him in.

Next morning he was gone again and I found from his tracks that he had crossed the road. That afternoon we tracked him to the point of exhaustion. He had wandered about in the most aimless manner. The snow was deep and the crust kept breaking at every other step. Finally we gave up.

'To hell with him,' I said at tea time. 'He was getting to be a bloody nuisance.'

'He's got Petruska bred anyway, at least I hope so,' said Beryl.

At dinner that night I remarked, 'I wonder where Peterkin is now?'

'Perhaps he's trying to get in again. He was a nice môose,' said Beryl.

'Yes, but you always liked Petruska best.'

'Well, you liked Peterkin best.'

'However,' said Beryl, 'it is really a relief to think that he won't be banging up people's cars. Anyway he knows where we are. He may come back in the fall to breed Petruska again.'

Next day there were no new tracks. Peterkin was gone and Petruska looked strangely deserted. It was a bad day and the only comfort was that the peahen's comb was recovering.

Three days later we drove out to see Dick Robinson of Adanac Films who produces animal films. A friend had told us about him and suggested that he might like to make use of our moose or of the game sanctuary for filming. We found him in, a grey-bearded white-headed man, smoking a short pipe, and wearing leather tasselled trousers and a leather tasselled coat. From his appearance I should have thought he was well over sixty but everything else about him belied this estimate. He was living in a corral of caravans and mobile homes surrounded by open air cages of bears, wolves, jaguars, foxes, coyotes, cougars and deer, all animals that he used or hoped to use for filming.

It turned out that he lived the parts that he was playing and since he had just produced a film about an old trapper and four wolves, 'Brothers of the Wind', he was currently an old trapper. He had been a young air observer in the war, so I suppose was still in his forties, certainly he moved like a man still in his forties, as he showed us around the animals. Every animal knew him, in fact he was obviously something special to them. He had a strong face with cool circumspect eyes, but if one looked carefully there was a lot of kindness there. That is what his animals undoubtedly recognized.

'I heard about you,' he said, 'I was wondering whether I could do anything sometime with your moose.'

'Well one of them's gone,' said Beryl.

'Oh no!' he said, 'What happened?'

Beryl told him and before we left he said, 'Let me know if you trace him and I'll bring out the whole gang. Float, capture gun, the lot, and we'll bring him home for you. I have a really good part for him if you find him . . .'

'What was that?' asked Beryl, interested.

'It goes like this,' said Dick, whose mind is always churning over new themes for filming. 'There's a woman living in the woods somewhere who has a reputation for being able to bring up wild animals. People bring her all kinds of wounded birds and deserted animals and one of the things that she has raised is a bull moose that she got as a calf.' It is probable that Dick had only just thought of this, but now his idea was away with him. He was having his troubles with the Fish and Wildlife Service over some question of permits. 'After the moose was two years old the Fish and Wildlife closed in on her and asked her why she hadn't a permit and while the officer is talking the moose comes up and horns his car. He has left it on top of a rise and it runs off down the hill and crashes into the stream.'

'Peterkin could do that without any training,' said Beryl.

It was late when we got back. Petruska was waiting for us by the house, still looking deserted and lonely. I put the car away and went upstairs, both of us thinking how sad it was that Peterkin had to go off just as a film career was being planned for him. Soon the telephone rang and when I answered it, a voice said 'This is Jack Reeve from about five miles north of you. I hear that you've lost a moose.'

'How did you know?'

'My brother's children have been over to the house and they told us. They got it from the Kerfoot boys at the school. I thought I'd ring you because there was a moose round the barn this evening and the children say they can still see him on the road below the house.'

'How do we get to you?'

'Take the Cremona road and come on up past the school, then turn left opposite the community hall. My farm is then the first on the left, a little off the road and up the hill. You'll see the lights. Take the first turning after you leave the Cremona road.'

'We'll be with you right away.' I turned to Beryl. 'They've seen Peterkin.'

'Where?' asked Beryl, already on her way downstairs for 'skidoo' suit, boots and gloves. It never occurred to us that it might not be Peterkin.

The night was bitter, at least twenty below, but there was no wind. We found the Reeves' farm without any difficulty, opened two high corral gates of a small 'holding area' through which the road passed, and drove up a heavily rutted and frozen track to the house. Jack Reeve and his wife welcomed us in to their warm kitchen.

'He was at my brother's haystacks yesterday,' he told us, 'but we would never have known about him if the children hadn't come to stay for the night while my brother was away to a cattle sale. They told us that you had lost a moose. He went down across the field there and on to the road but he has gone now.'

'We'll go and see if we can find him. Have you got a barn if we get him back?'

'I can turn the cows out. They won't come to any harm. One of them is due to calve but she'll be all right.'

'Well, we don't know whether we can get him, but it's very kind of you.'

Beryl and I drove back on to the road and soon picked up Peterkin's tracks in the snow. There were other moose tracks too which led to a small haystack beside the road. The country was much more wooded here and it looked as if Peterkin might have met another moose. It was a moonlit night and the trees stood black and still against the snow. We presently discovered that Peterkin had jumped the wire fence on the side of the road and wandered off to the north. At least we hoped that it was Peterkin.

'I'll go after him,' said Beryl, 'you had better stay hadn't you?'

I have always done everything with Beryl or she with me, but the snow was deep with a crust that broke and I knew that I would be more of a hindrance than a help.

'We'll keep calling,' I told her. 'It isn't the sort of night to go walking by oneself in the woods in this cold. Don't go far from the road and if I can't hear you I shall come after you.'

Beryl set off through the trees. At least she was wearing the right clothes and boots but she would have been better off with snow shoes. She had soon disappeared calling as she went 'Peterkin, Peterkin'; her voice sounded through the otherwise silent night getting always further away. In the intervals between her calls there was nothing to be heard, no sound of wind, no rustle of snow falling from a branch, no owl's hoot, no distant motor. Now I stood still not daring to move lest I should lose the sound of her voice. I imagined her like some forest bird flying away and calling, the call growing fainter and more distant. And then, as if she had been a curlew on some upland whose lonely call suddenly changes to a ripple of new notes, I heard a change in her voice and knew at once that she had found Peterkin.

Ten minutes later I heard her coming back and talking as she came in a conversational way to Peterkin; soon they were coming through the trees. Beryl was making remarkably light work of the heavy going and behind her came a tall shadow stalking slowly and elegantly, a dignitary coming down a red carpet, a bishop of the woods pacing the cathedral aisle of trees.

'Hello Peterkin,' I said, more pleased than I could ever have imagined I'd be to see him again. 'How did you find him?'

'He was so nice,' she said, 'I was just calling and following his tracks. Then I'd wait for a moment. Suddenly I heard him blow his nose, and out he came. He walked straight up to me and pushed his nose into my face. I think he was very glad to see me.'

We walked back together and Peterkin jumped over the barbed wire fence on to the road. He followed Beryl down the road, while I drove the car behind and far enough away not to upset him.

Back at the farm we opened the gate of the holding area. Peterkin was now safely inside a high rail fence, the top rail about five feet high. We could not take him into the barn where there were high doors because the cattle that had been turned out were standing round it. Peterkin was obviously nervous of them and we would have had to bring him out of the collecting area so that he might easily have gone off again. By keeping within the farm fence we could take him to the other end of the barn and with the help of the tall young farmer tried to drive him through a door, but it was too low and Peterkin, who had a most delicate sense of smell, now smelt either pigs or cattle, and had no intention of entering. At this end of the barn there was a corral, also made of poles with the top rail five feet high. 'Why not put him in there till

you get something to take him away in?' suggested Jack
Reeve. 'There is a loading platform there too.' The gate was
opened and Peterkin went in happily. We then walked down
the hill and across to the house. Peterkin followed us inside
the rails of the corral and when he got to the bottom side he
jumped over them almost without hesitation. A moose stands
very tall. He only has to rear up and with quite a moderate
jump he can clear five feet. Unlike a horse he does not pick up
his hind legs to clear an obstacle. He seems to forget about
them and they just follow on behind.

Leaving Peterkin we went into the house to telephone Dick
and ask for his assistance in getting Peterkin home. It was some
time before we were able to locate him, as he had gone to the
hospital to see his newly born daughter. Without any hesitation he said that he'd bring out his people, and I arranged to
meet them on the highway and show them the way. While we
were telephoning there was a loud twang from the side of the
house and we discovered that Peterkin had removed the
clothes line that was fastened there.

I left Beryl to entertain Peterkin and went off to meet Dick.
It had taken him longer than he had expected to organize his
army and I had a cold wait at the crossroads unable to keep
the car warm as I was low on fuel. They arrived soon after
midnight and made a most impressive sight. Including Dick,
who led the procession, there were about five vehicles and
eight men, all dressed in skidoo suits with the Adanac Film
Company's badge on the arm. It looked like some war-time
meeting at the crossroads. We drove off keeping a regular
military distance between vehicles. There was no doubt that
Dick liked to do things in style. They were equipped with
ropes and capture gun and I felt that Peterkin was already as
good as in the float.

We drove up to the collecting area gates, then stopped the

convoy, while Dick and I walked up to the house. I could see no sign of Peterkin and had an empty feeling that all was not well. Beryl opened the door, 'I'm so sorry,' she said, 'he's gone.'

Dick took this announcement without a tremor.

'We got him into the collecting area again,' Beryl explained, 'and he was down by the water trough. I kept feeding him bread. I couldn't feed him bread continuously and it was so bitterly cold that I kept coming up to the house, to get warm and then going down with more bread. Well he must have got bored, for he just jumped over the water trough and a double stand of wire behind it and he's gone off to the wood. I thought it was all right to leave him because the rails are much higher there and I never thought he'd jump over the water trough.'

There was nothing more to be done that night and we all returned to our house, to some 'bad weather' soup that Beryl used to make on the yacht, and a glass of wine. Everyone was soon feeling better.

'Tomorrow,' said Dick, 'we'll locate him. We'll have a proper operation, bring out the skidoos, and really cover the country. See you tomorrow.' The black-suited army withdrew. 'He's got a really good lot of people,' I said to Beryl. 'You know, morale, discipline, enthusiasm and all that. They seem to be an excellent outfit.'

I had another date next day that prevented me going out on the hunt, but the film company picked up Beryl and spent the whole day searching. The trouble was that there were too many moose tracks and it was impossible to say 'this is Peterkin, this is the way he has gone.' They met many farmers all of whom showed an interest in the recovery of the moose. It seemed that our moose were better known in the country-side than we had thought. 'You want to get him in again,' was the general theme, 'otherwise he's bound to get shot.'

Beryl met Jack Reeve's brother who had seen the moose the night before we had so nearly got him. 'He was at my haystacks,' he said. 'He really looked like a lost moose to me. He didn't seem to be able to make up his mind where he was going. Most moose we see know what they are doing but this was a lost one.'

They were back in the evening and none the wiser except that it seemed most likely that he had gone north.

Dick and his men came in for more soup and cheese and as they left Dick said, 'There's only one thing to do. Hire a helicopter and find him from the air, and then you'll have to bulldoze the snow away from the fence, and weld five foot extensions to the posts so that you can heighten the wire where it drifts.' All this would cost far more than Peterkin was worth if we sold him, which we didn't intend to do anyway. He was becoming a liability. Dick saw the look on our faces at the contemplation of all this expense.

'If you like,' he said, 'I'll do it all. But if I get him he's my moose. He can go on staying here and breed Petruska, but he'll be my moose.' No agreement was ever concluded more quickly.

Next morning a reduced party from Adanac Films joined us with a float and we waited at the house while Dick went off, not in a helicopter, but in a light aircraft, to try and find Peterkin. Presently an aircraft flew low over the house, turned and made another pass. As it came over, Dick threw a message wrapped in his coat, but threw it so accurately that it landed on the roof. The aircraft was flying so low approaching from the south, that we, on the north side of the house were unable to see the coat thrown out, since the roof of the house screened them until they were over us. The aircraft then flew off to the airfield for small aircraft about twenty miles to the south-east. An hour later Dick joined us.

'Didn't you get my message?' he asked, 'it's right on the roof of the house,' but what really upset him was that when his coat was recovered from the roof, his pipe that had been in the pocket was gone.

They had discovered the moose lying down on a hill about ten miles to the north in an aspen wood. Fortunately, since there were no leaves on the trees, any game had been easy to see. Near him they had seen three mule deer. Dick had taken Pat, one of his young people with him, who had put himself through college by working a trap line, and was a good tracker. We all set off now for a farm below the hill where the moose had been seen. A field road led to it where the snow was deep and the track icy but we all made it successfully. An old farmer lived there by himself, his small farmhouse as neat as could be. I told him about the moose and asked him if he had a barn that I could get the moose into if we got him down. He had a small hay barn with high double doors.

Beryl and Pat, the tracker, set off through deep snow, each step breaking through a foot or more, and disappeared in the woods behind the house. They climbed the hill and after half an hour came upon three mule deer, still sitting in the trees where they had been seen from the aircraft. 'Those are the deer we saw,' Pat said, 'now he must be somewhere near.'

Beryl was following behind Pat who was breaking trail. 'Shall I start calling now?' she asked.

Pat nodded. 'Yes, you go ahead now.'

'No fear,' Beryl said, 'if I call he'll think it's me anyway. You go on breaking trail and I'll go ahead when I see him.' She started calling and from away over the hill and through the still trees I could hear her. They seemed to have moved quickly and were some way south so I made my way back to the barn and waited.

Up on the hill Pat and Beryl were following a seismic line, a bulldozed track running up hill and down dale as straight as if it had been ruled. They are made along grid lines in the search for oil and gas. Pat, stamping on ahead, suddenly stopped and pointed. 'Is that your moose?' he asked. Beryl looked ahead and saw a moose standing on the edge of the cleared line about two hundred yards away. His head was against some dark fir trees so that she could not distinguish his horns.

'It looks like him,' she said doubtfully.

They walked on with Beryl now leading. The track went into a small hollow and they lost sight of the moose. When she came up on the next rise he was gone. 'Peterkin, Peterkin,' she called, her breath white on the frosty air, 'Peterkin, Peterkin,' as she looked along the side of the line which he had been facing. 'Peterkin, Peterkin.'

Suddenly she heard Pat ask again in excitement, 'Is this your moose?' Turning she saw a moose on the other side of the track and just in the trees stalking boldly towards her. It was Peterkin. Beryl walked towards him and as they met, from his superior height he stretched out his nose, his big brown nose with a small triangle of brown bare skin just in the middle above the lip, and she gave him a kiss. Then he nuzzled her hair.

'Look what I've got for you,' she said, producing a cellophane wrapped loaf of sliced 'Dutch oven' 60 per cent whole wheat bread, and Peterkin took a slice greedily.

'Thank God,' said Pat, 'that it's the right moose. We saw another moose lying five miles to the north, but we thought that the nearest would be the most likely. I didn't like to tell you, but when I saw this character so close and coming on like that, I sure felt nervous.'

Peterkin was pleased to see Beryl but he did not like Pat, and started to put his ears back and roll his eyes, placing himself between Pat and Beryl and interfering with Pat's progress in his usual way by getting in front and then whirling round with his head down.

'You'd better go on and send Miles up,' said Beryl. 'I'll bring him on slowly.'

'What happens if he runs after me?' asked Pat, still unsure of Peterkin's behaviour.

'Well don't run. He'll be all right.'

Pat left with hurried short steps going as fast as he could without actually running. He met me at the barn. 'Your wife wants you up there,' he said, 'he's being a bit strange.'

They were still some way away from the farm when I met them. Beryl, looking very small beside Peterkin, had reached up and was walking with her hand on his neck. On account of Peterkin's slow and stately pace they reminded me of an elderly and very dignified gentleman taking his grandchild for a walk on a winter's day.

Peterkin and I sniffed noses and then I walked ahead while Beryl, still with her hand on his neck, walked beside him. We went straight to the barn, and as we went, saw that Dick and his team were discreetly hidden behind trucks and cars. I opened the doors of the barn and Peterkin walked in with Beryl without any reluctance. I followed them in and shut the doors. There had been no animals in the barn and the only smell was of hay. We gave Peterkin a feed-bowl of his Moose Pellets and he went down on his knees to eat them. Moose usually go on their knees to eat off the ground, rather than straddling their legs like a giraffe.

We backed the trailer, on which was a large plywood and iron bound crate, to the barn doors. It was just big enough to hold Peterkin.

'He'll never go in with the roof on,' said Beryl, and the roof was taken off.

'Now,' suggested Dick, 'suppose you go inside and persuade him to follow you in. Then we can shut the door.'

'But how do I get out,' asked Beryl.

'I thought you might climb out over the front.'

I expected all hell to break loose the moment that we shut the door, for Peterkin's gentle manners would make one inclined to forget that he is still a wild animal and a very powerful one. 'Absolutely no,' I said, 'she really can't be shut in with him.'

'Then she'll have to stand on the trailer bar,' said Dick.

'But I can't begin to see over the top of the crate,' said Beryl.

A forty-five gallon drum was put on the trailer bar and Beryl stood on this. The sliding barn doors were opened to the width of the crate, and the open crate door and the crate roof were held so as to make a passage. Peterkin, being used to me, did not mind my standing holding the door and I could see him through the crack between it and the barn doors. Dick and his team stood behind the crate roof, forming the other side of the passage, ready to put it on as soon as I had shut the door on Peterkin. All that Peterkin could see of them were the black fingers of their gloved hands, holding the roof up as a wall. These he regarded with deep suspicion. Beryl started to call him and to tempt him with the feed bucket, but he had never been in a trailer before. He kept stepping up and stepping down. Once he had three legs in and then backed out again. I could see what was going on and could speak to Peterkin, but one could almost feel the excitement behind the crate roof and in the tense black fingers holding it in place. I was excited enough myself and imagined that it might be communicated to Peterkin. At last he stepped right in and I shut the door and almost before he was aware of this the bolts were fast.

For a moment there was silence. Then like a huge jack-in-a-box Peterkin rose out of the top of the crate and for a moment he towered over Beryl. His forelegs were out and over the side. We gave futile shouts of 'No, Peterkin, no.' It looked as if he was going to topple over, but before he could give the final push to his teetering balance, his hind legs slipped and he sat down in the crate. Dick's team went into action as if they had a tiger there and in no time the roof was on and fastened down with chains, while the door rang with several powerful kicks and the whole trailer rocked with Peterkin's struggle. We were ready to start for home but the solitary old farmer had made tea. 'You can't go away like that, damn it,' he called, 'the tea's on.'

'We'll have to go,' I said to Beryl, nothing loath as far as I was concerned.

We trooped into the neat little house leaving Dick to check over the trailer fastenings. 'Come on, Old Timer,' shouted the farmer, who was at least thirty years older than Dick, but had noticed his white hair and beard, his woollen hat, tasselled coat and doeskin trousers. The tea was excellent and from the state of the crockery and the table it was hard to believe that there wasn't a woman there too. The Old Timer had barely sat down when the crate began to rock with Peterkin's new efforts.

'I'll have to get the show on the road to keep him quiet,' said Dick and half an hour later we were back at our home. Peterkin backed out seeming none the worse for his adventure. He looked round, made no attempt to move away, and then followed Beryl round to the feed trough. She called Petruska and then put some feed in the trough.

When Peterkin saw Petruska he put his ears forward in a foolish welcoming look, but Petruska ignored him. She cut him as if he weren't there and started feeding. Peterkin turned his attention again to the trough and the moment he started eating Petruska wheeled on him and struck him such a violent blow with her foreleg that Peterkin left the feed, making his protesting bleat.

Later on she came round to the back of the house where

Peterkin had gone, and then pinned back her ears and with rolling eyes advanced on him, reared up, and struck him with both her forelegs. It was obvious that she was telling him that he had no right to leave her in her present condition, for although there were as yet no visible signs, she was in calf. For a day or two Peterkin seemed to surrender his authority but they were soon back to normal, Peterkin having once more assumed the role of the dominant male.

Petruska had never behaved like this before, nor as far as we know did she do it again, until she was about to have her calf, and wanted to be left in peace and solitude.

7. An Elk arrives

The first time we went to see Dick Robinson in his encampment of animals surrounded by fir trees and under snowy peaks with the frozen river just below, he showed us a young elk standing by itself in the centre of a large round wire cage, with two hairy knobs on his brow from which would soon sprout his first single spikes. He stood with his hocks touching and slightly bent as if he felt the cold. In his large brown eyes there was a look of revolt against the fate that had put him there, the expression of a small boy standing in the nursery corner.

'He's no good,' Dick told us. 'I got him too late and we can't do anything with him. He sometimes strikes at whoever is trying to feed him. You can have him if you like. We'll probably end by eating him. He is called Larry.'

We had got our moose because they were individually endangered although not an endangered species. Here was another animal specifically in danger of being eaten. Dick rarely spoke of an animal like this though he had a wolf there that he also condemned as being no good.

'What do you mean "No good," ' Beryl had asked, referring to the wolf.

'Can't trust him,' said Dick. 'They're born like that. Some are good, some are mean. Like people. Not like this one,' he said, turning to a big wolf that was fawning and whining at the cage door. He opened the cage door, let the wolf out and wrestled with it. Then he let it go and it ran off to lift its leg against the posts of the fence that enclosed the cages. When it was time to shut it up again it behaved like any dog, rolling on its back and pleading until it was finally hustled back into the cage. 'They all come out regularly for exercise, but not that other one. I couldn't begin to fool about with him. He'd probably go for me and then beat it. I shall have to sell him to a zoo or something.'

Before we left, Beryl and I had a quick consultation. 'If you really want to get rid of that elk, we'll take him,' she offered. 'All right. I'll bring him round to you some time,' he replied.

It was about a month after Peterkin's return that Dick Robinson arrived with the elk in a trailer. He had brought a movie camera and had hoped to get a picture of the elk's arrival and his reception by the moose. The country was about as bleak as it could be. The drive was muddy and snow was lying at the back of the house and in hollows and patches in the fields. The only sign of spring was an occasional gopher on the side of the road or at the mouth of its burrow, or the wide spread of an eagle's wings soaring over Grand Valley. The eagles, both golden and bald, are the first harbingers of spring and can be seen in the valley from about 7 March until the first week in April. There was no sign of green anywhere, no leaf on the trees and the grass dead and brown. A bad day for filming and as it happened there was little to film.

The elk came out of his trailer and looked about him in some surprise at his apparent freedom. He stepped slowly and suspiciously, head erect and ears forward, towards the front of the house. The moose, always alert to what is going on, were soon on the scene and it looked as if we were all set to record their meeting. Suddenly Kochi, belatedly aware that strangers had arrived, came running round the house, barking as she ran and putting on an additional show because she had been caught napping. The elk threw back his head as if he had a large spread of antlers to carry and galloped away, followed full tilt by the moose and Kochi. Kochi stopped as we shouted to her, the moose a little later, but the elk kept on running until he disappeared in the trees.

'Well,' said Dick, 'there goes Larry and that's the end of filming for today. I wish you joy of him, but I doubt whether you will get much of it.'

That evening Beryl said, 'We can't call him Larry. Larry the Elk. It sounds like a child's story. I shall have to find him another name.'

The next day, although the moose appeared, there was no sign of the elk. We found his tracks along the side of the fence and could see that he had been exploring. We put some hay out for him in front of the house. It was five days before we saw him again. Then the moose appeared with a self-conscious, prideful look on their faces, as if to say, 'Look what we have found.' Behind them came the elk. The cow moose put her head down and took some hay. The bull has to go down on his knees to take anything from the ground, perhaps because he is taller, perhaps because his neck in comparison is a little shorter in order later to carry the great weight of his horns. He disdained to stoop in front of the elk and took some hay from Petruska's mouth. Neither of them enjoy hay anyway; they only push it around with their noses, like children searching in a bran tub, expecting to find something inside. They did not like the elk to feed with them, but had no objecting to his eating behind.

In the evening they all appeared again with the elk still following behind the moose. He was given his pellets in a separate feed trough and came up suspiciously with his head held high and one forefoot raised as he halted between steps. As he did this he curled his upper lip in a supercilious way as if to say that the pellets were inferior to the food that he was used to and that he was not accustomed to being served without a cloth.

'He behaves in such a prissy way,' said Beryl, 'in fact that is what I'm going to call him.'

'I don't see much difference between that and Larry,' I protested, thinking of something more imposing like 'Prince' or 'Royal' as the big farm horses used to be called in their day.

'Well that's his name,' she decided.

On 27 March, a fateful day for Prissy, he arrived with the moose in the morning and came towards Beryl with his usual mincing tread, stopping to raise a foot and curling his upper lip as he approached her. When she put the food down in front of him he struck at her with a foreleg, grazing her arm. Beryl was furious but she had nothing with which to deal with him.

When he arrived again in the evening she held a short length of iron pipe in her hand. He came up to the food trough and, went through the same procedure, which is in fact a challenge, a desire for dominance. If he wished to dominate Beryl he learned his lesson as she struck him smartly on the nose. He went off shaking his head but soon returned in a conciliatory manner for his feed. Beryl never forgave him fully, never trusted him again, and although she changed the iron pipe for a length of rubber hose, she never went near him without something in her hand.

Prissy bore no ill will but as a result of his aggression he was never fed bread by hand as the moose were, for it brought him into striking distance with the feeder. Our moose, except when the cow is with her calves and cannot come, are only fed in front of the house so that if we meet them in the woods they are not disappointed when they get no food. After their feed at the house they are given bread, like candy, but they are not in the least upset if they don't get it. An elk, more volatile and aggressive than the moose, if not given food when he has learnt to expect it, might turn on his dilatory host in disappointment. The regimen has to be stricter for them.

One December day, when the moose were still yearlings, two young men came from the Zoo to cut a Christmas tree. One of them was kneeling under the tree, chopping away just above the root, when the bull moose thrust his head under the low branches from the other side. The young man was out from under the tree like a startled rabbit, brandishing his axe in preparation for self-defence. I thought that he had over-reacted, but it turned out that he had recently come out of hospital after being skewered by an elk while throwing hay to it over its fence. The elk had charged him and caught him against his truck which was near to the fence. One of the tines of the antlers went into his chest, passing close to his heart. No wonder he had quick reactions.

Although Prissy had sown the seeds of distrust in our hearts, he knew nothing of this. Whatever his future it was far better for the time being than the confinement of his cage. After his feed that evening he played for some time with the bull in the marsh below the house, the moose being more interested in sex and the elk in play. At dark they were all sitting in front of the glass doors of the living room.

From the time Beryl hit Prissy he seemed to be fully accepted by the moose, perhaps in sympathetic understanding for the blow that he had received. They were usually seen in a troop together. The bull and Prissy often sparred together, but as Peterkin still had his horns and those of Prissy were only budding, he took care not to get too close.

Peterkin lost his first horn on 11 April. Young moose keep their horns much longer than old moose, who may drop their horns as early as the end of January. We discovered Kochi gnawing at the newly shed horn and as I already had a single horn dropped by a whitetail I put it and the moose's horn on one of the beams of the downstairs living room to make a bracket for my old cavalry sword. Peterkin dropped his second horn on the following day but we only found it two years later when Kochi's puppy was seen gnawing at it. The lost horns left two sockets on his brow about half an inch deep, which looked raw and painful, but within a day they had scabbed over and within a week they were filled with new growth.

The moose and the elk continued to move about together and usually arrived together at feed time. Feed consisted of a scoop of herbivore pellets once a day, a total of two pounds each. For the rest the moose had to depend on aspen and willow twigs on which they browsed untidily. The elk did some browsing too, but he also grazed off the old dead grass. All three looked in splendid condition in spite of their twiggy diet.

If the two males arrived by themselves at feed time, they had to wait for Petruska so that they might all feed together. This was the only way to ensure that she got her feed, which, particularly when in calf, we thought she needed, without being molested. If Peterkin arrived first we used to ask him, 'Where is Petruska?' Moose seem to know most things that are going on within a mile of them, but they are vulnerable to hunters because they mistake man's heavy progress through the bush, the brushing of twigs and the breaking of sticks, for the movement of another moose and either stay to investigate or come out to challenge. When asked where Petruska was, Peterkin would slowly turn his head and prick his big ears in her direction. Almost invariably she'd soon appear, plucking at the bushes as she wandered slowly towards the house until she saw the others at the feed trough. Then she'd break into her swift trot.

One evening both appeared without Petruska.

'Where's Petruska?' asked Beryl.

They both looked to the north along the east side of the drive. After half an hour Petruska was still missing.

'I won't feed you without Petruska,' Beryl told them.

Prissy looked at Peterkin and then went off towards the north. He disappeared in the trees, leaving Peterkin waiting patiently like the farmer's cob I used to see on market day outside the pub, when I was a boy in Yorkshire. Presently Prissy returned. Living in close contact with animals there is a tendency to believe that they have greater powers of understanding or communication than perhaps they have. Now Prissy seemed to say to the moose: 'I can't do anything with her. You have a go.'

In his turn Peterkin moved off ponderously into the trees to the north while Prissy waited impatiently at the feed trough. The few weeks that he had been with us had already had a great effect on his appearance. He had filled out and his coat was looking better, legs, head and neck dark brown, body sandy, a reddish brown backside and the beginnings of a shaggy mane under his neck. He stood by the trough, head erect, ears and eyes directed towards the edge of the woods where Peterkin had disappeared, looking like any hungry person anxiously awaiting the coming of dinner.

Presently Peterkin appeared closely followed by Petruska.

As the time for calving approached, if indeed Petruska was

going to have a calf, she spent more time by herself, chewing the cud in front of the house. 'I'm sure that if she has a calf, she'll have it right here,' said Beryl. 'The Boys', as they were sometimes called were thrown more on their own resources. They wandered together and played together and sometimes quarrelled. Then, since they had no horns, they stood up and boxed. Prissy was a great 'stand-upper' and could remain with his nose in the air standing straight on his hind legs for at least a minute, or at any rate for as long as it took us to find the camera, but never long enough for us to get a picture. Peterkin was taller and had more weight, but his blows rarely found a target. On the other hand if Petruska took such action she meant business and both 'the Boys' understood it. Yet, although she was beginning to object to Peterkin's company, she did not seem to mind the elk hanging round. Peterkin now was rarely with her, the elk often.

8. Petruska's Calf

It was the beginning of April and the only change about the countryside was in the arrival of the birds. The eagles come first and by the end of March the red-tailed hawks arrive. The most notable feature of bird life in this part of the country is the hawks. The great red-tail is perhaps the most common, but there are many others: Swainson's and the marsh hawk are the ones that I see most often.

March is the back end of winter and spring is still a long way away, with no leaves or grass until May. Cold bleak April, when we still have snow-falls and sometimes wonder if anything will ever grow again, is alive with migrating birds so that we cannot help feeling that they, like the calves in the fields, have better news than we. Through all the cold winter we have had the chickadees and the hairy and downy woodpeckers round the house, busy at the fat hung on the trees in front of the windows. It had to be hung high enough to prevent the elk from eating it; he seemed to enjoy the fat as much as the birds. Now the cheery 'dee dee dee' of the chickadees has gone back somewhere into the woods where the insects are already stirring in the bark of trees. The woodpeckers also have vanished, soon to be replaced by the flickers and the sapsuckers.

Suddenly there are sparrows in the barn. The crows arrive and on 4 April for the last three years the first starlings have appeared sitting in the trees behind the house. They are the newcomers from the east and are said to have chased away the bluebirds. They come in April in flocks, but I have not found them nesting here. In September they are about again, increased in numbers by their drab brown young. Just about the time that the moose lost his horns there were pintail and mallard sitting on the ice that still partially covered the lake. Then came a pair of goldeneye and on 15 April the first yelping whistling swans passed in a swaying skein of a hundred or more, low over the house. Next day between forty and fifty mallard were sitting on the ice.

On that day we had a visitor, a tall and powerfully built young man called Garry. He wore glasses and his dark hair in a bob to the nape of his neck. He had recently been on a trip to France, Italy, Yugoslavia, Greece, Hungary, England and Ireland and made penetrating comments on them all. Hungary he had liked most and Ireland least, perhaps because he had been thrown out of a pub in Dublin.

Garry had been brought up for the most part of his not too long life on his grandfather's farm in Ontario. From there he had gone north on a survey team in the Arctic and when this closed down he came south to Calgary. As he passed the kitchens of the Palliser Hotel a marvellous smell of fresh bread and a rush of warm air came out of an open door. It made such an impression on the young man back from the Arctic that he walked in and got a job as an apprentice baker. When we met him he was second baker to the Palliser and capable of baking excellent French bread, amongst many other things. Life in town was not for him but he had left school too early and had to make a living with his hands. He asked if he could come out and do work for us when he had a day off.

'We'd love to have you,' I said, since we had both taken to him, 'but as you see, this is all do-it-yourself here. We couldn't pay you anything.'

'Oh Lord,' he said, 'I didn't mean that. It's for my own sake. I just want to get out to the country and do some work to get rid of that town feeling.'

For the next eighteen months he came almost every Sunday night and left on Tuesday evening, often bringing a warm French roll with him. He never seemed happier than when he had a job to do, particularly with the animals. He was quiet when other people were around, but talked well with us, and since we did not take a local newspaper we relied on him for the local news. Like all Canadians he seemed a bit touched in the head about hockey, which the English call ice hockey, and the only alterations to his regular visits were when there was a hockey game in Calgary, Lethbridge, or Red Deer, which he had to visit, or when he went on his holiday to the mountains.

Garry's regular appearances soon made a big difference to the work that we were doing and we found ourselves putting off the harder tasks until he arrived. One of the jobs that is always with us is collecting stones from the half section and bringing them to the game sanctuary. We use the large ones for building the wall to keep the moose off the terrace and the smaller ones for building islands in the pond so that the duck may have safer nesting. They are also used for making a cobbled drive at the back of the house so that when the moose or elk for some reason are put in the driveway they will leave the house alone. The three of them do not like walking on cobbles; neither for that matter do our visitors, but perhaps one day the stones will sink deep enough to allow easier access, and by then the animals will have learned to avoid them.

The wall in front of the terrace has now reached the proportions of an old Mashona fortification on top of a hill in Rhodesia, that is to say nothing very much. Some of the stones must weigh over two hundred pounds. These are known as Garry stones.

By the end of April we had had most of the duck that pass through in the pond and also our summer residents. We had scaup, pintail, mallard, an odd canvasback and redhead, green- and blue-winged teal, bufflehead, ring-necked duck and American widgeon. We also had western grebe, red-necked grebe, and eared grebe. The snipe had arrived, one loon, the greater yellowlegs and a white-winged scoter. The population was always changing. I heard the first snipe drumming on 1 May, a deeper note than the wild vibration that I had so often heard in marshy places in England but just as exciting. One day a snipe slid past the window as it glided to the swamp just below the house, still drumming. I never knew that they would or could make the noise so close to their landing. They drummed at any time of the day, but usually in the morning or evening and sometimes on a moonlit night.

The only physical changes that we could see in Petruska during her pregnancy were that the sockets above her eyes became deeper and her face looked leaner, but on 11 May when she came to her feed there was no doubt that she was going to have a calf. Even then her shape showed no trace that she was carrying one, but her backside, under her diminutive tail, was looking moist, broader and relaxed. On the 14th no one came to the house and the next day we saw her walking purposefully down the fence towards the corner by the pond. She did not come when called, but when Peterkin and Prissy arrived, cutting across from the fence and avoiding the corner, Petruska changed her mind and joined them. She looked as if she was ready to calve that night, but I could see no signs of milk in her udder.

On 17 May, the 225th day after we thought that she had been bred, she stayed away from the house. She didn't appear next day, or the next, but Peterkin and Prissy came, the former with two long scrapes on his shoulder as if he had been struck by Petruska's sharp hooves. On the third day Peterkin hung about the house and Beryl, who was convinced that he was upset about something, petted him. It was obvious that there had been some disruption in his life and he needed comfort.

We were sure now that Petruska had calved. Professor Geist, of Calgary University, one of the greatest experts on moose, had advised us not to worry but to wait until she brought the calf to us. We did not need pressing. People who have spent a great deal of their time in the Canadian woods are apt to say that they would rather meet a grizzly on a narrow path than come suddenly on a cow moose and her calf. Peterkin's scars were evidence of what she might do. We did not worry anyway because spring had arrived with a bang, the aspens all in fresh green leaf and the willows and birch scrub in the same state. The young green grass was showing through the old brown, flattened by the winter's snow. It seemed a good time for the moose to have her calf now that the birds were singing and all the trees were in succulent leaf. Nature could well look after her own.

It was not until the 29th that we saw her and her calf. Just before breakfast we saw a moose walking between the pond and the fence towards the corner that Petruska had seemed to fancy earlier. Beryl ran down the path and called to her. She looked round for a moment and then ran off into the trees and bushes in the corner. Running close behind her, looking in the distance like a yellow labrador behind a horse, was a small but apparently very active calf.

The peacocks were now living by the house and during the next few nights their water was finished completely by something that came in during the night. We began to think that it was Petruska coming round and hoping for some feed. We saw the calf again on 9 June. They were both some way away but Petruska pricked her ears when Beryl called and seemed much more relaxed. The week after, we saw Petruska, followed by her calf and Prissy, making her way towards her corner by the pond. Suddenly she turned and attacked Prissy with her forefeet, chasing him away.

Peterkin had been much alone for the past few weeks. He had taken a dislike to Prissy, who finally got the message and tried to force himself on Petruska. When Prissy found that he wasn't wanted there either he sulked by himself for a day or two, then made up his quarrel with Peterkin. No doubt they discussed Petruska's strange behaviour and how badly they had been treated. Although Peterkin continued to keep well away from Petruska, Prissy still could not believe that he wasn't wanted. Elk are more of a herd animal than moose. He continued to hang around Petruska until finally she seemed to accept him although she would not let Peterkin near.

It was over a month before we made contact with her. A few days before, the solitary Peterkin had appeared with a fore fetlock full of porcupine quills. After three or four sessions and much plaintive 'hey heying' we managed to get them all out, but Beryl began to worry about a porcupine and the calf.

Some years ago the former owner of this place had pushed a lot of aspen down in order to sow barley. The dead trunks were piled high ready for burning but had never been burnt. All the land cleared had been left as it was so that the young aspen had grown thickly all over the cleared area, providing wonderful forage for the moose, but the piles of grey trunks and dead branches made a refuge for porcupines, and when the snow came, a regular home for them.

The trunks provided free boarding-houses also for squirrels and rabbits, for a bobcat perhaps and in the summer all kinds of birds; wrens in particular made use of them. We had not burnt the logs for fear of damaging the trees around or even of cooking a porcupine, but now something had to be done about them. In one woodpile I had seen a porcupine and her young slowly entering by a well-worn path as if they carried a load of grief with them. I thought of them as a widow and her daughter, in untidy black, bowed with sorrow and returning to an empty hearth. Not the sort of people one would willingly set fire to. Beryl suggested that Garry and I should pull their house to pieces, stacking the wood where it could be burnt, and remove the inmates to some other place several miles away. Armed with a large rubbish bin and a long-handled spade for guiding porcupines we set off for the eviction.

We were pulling the woodpile to pieces when I heard the sound of a big animal pushing through the brush. Suddenly I caught sight of Petruska quite close, with her ears back, forcing her way through some thick willows.

'Go away, get off,' I said to Garry, not knowing what Petruska's actions might be but principally mindful of the many warnings that we had received; 'tell Beryl that Petruska's here.'

Garry looked reluctant to leave me and indeed if there had to be a hassle with a cow moose there was no one whom I would rather have with me, but as Petruska pushed out of the bushes she put her big ears forward and I realized that they had only been back because of the scrub. She looked perfectly relaxed and friendly, but to begin with I took care to have the brush pile between us. I began to talk to her but she looked anxiously towards the house as if there was another voice she wished to hear. We started making our way there together and presently she heard it. 'Petruska, Petrooska,' came the distant cry. Petruska pricked her ears, broke immediately into a run, and soon disappeared in the direction of the house.

There followed a happy reunion and the moose soon finished a whole loaf of bread. She went back with Beryl to the house and took a little more feed, but we had started the fencing of the drive and there were strangers about so that she soon became nervous, and wandered off in quite a different direction to that from which she had arrived. Beryl, contrary to her earlier decision, had put some ointment on the fly sores above her hocks. She stopped to remove every trace of the ointment by careful licking and then went on her way, stopping first at the salt block which we put out for the moose and then pulling haphazardly at a few bushes.

'I wonder if she's lost her calf,' said Beryl.

She came again that evening and as she was taking her feed I had a look at her bag. There was plenty of milk there but it was not distended. Apart from the fly sores she was in good condition but lame in the shoulder. Beryl decided that she had done this driving off the bull. One has to blame the man for something and I don't think there was any real justification for this assumption.

'I'll walk off in the direction she came from,' I told Beryl. 'Perhaps I'll see the calf, but anyway you stay and see if she looks worried.' Petruska looked mildly after me as she chewed her pellets and showed no sign of anxiety. She hung around for some time and then wandered away as if with no set purpose.

The day after we had made contact with Petruska and while

we were still worrying about the calf, Beryl found them both in a swamp and got a good close view. 'It's so stocky,' she kept telling me, 'nothing like Petruska was when we got her.' The calf ran away but Petruska waited for a short time and then went off slowly in the same direction.

The following day, when Beryl was wandering along one of the moose paths and calling gently, she heard the quiet cough that moose always make when they want to tell you that they are there. Turning round she saw the cow and calf following close behind her. As she turned round the calf ran off a short distance, but Petruska came up licking her lips. Beryl gave her some bread until Petruska became anxious and started looking round for her calf which was standing a short way off behind a bush. Beryl left them and the cow stood still watching her go.

From now on we walked every day in the woods in order to give Petruska her feed and to get on better terms with the calf. July is a wonderful month. The prairie flowers are all in bloom and the open places, particularly along the grassy lane to the pond, are bright with harebells and shootingstars, with numerous kinds of milkvetch, with pink three flowered avens and blue lupins. In the woods the most distinctive flowers are the paintbrushes and the western wood lily, the beautiful red and black spotted lily that must not be plucked for it soon dies and will not grow again from that place. It was lovely to walk through the woods in all their green amongst the shadow-dappled grey trunks, so open compared with the dark rain forest of the coast, dry underfoot yet carpeted with grass, with here and there a red lily; to walk in anticipation of meeting the moose and her calf and suddenly to find the elk close behind, his single spikes well grown and velvet-covered; or to hear a cough and find the bull moose behind, tall and solemn, stalking silently, with his horns growing so fast that if you missed him for a day or two you were always surprised to see the way that they had spread.

One day, when Beryl was on her prowl through the woods, the bull moose, ears back and eyes rolling, burst out of some bushes and rushed towards her. The cow moose, also with her ears back, was close behind. For a moment Beryl thought that they were protecting the calf and that she was the object of the attack. But they brushed past her and she saw that it was the bull who had been attacked. Petruska gave him a parting punch on the quarters and then came back to Beryl. She was slightly out of breath, licking her lips, as it were wiping her hands on her apron. This was the first real intimation that as far as we were concerned the cow had no anxiety about us and her calf, for during the pursuit she had left the calf virtually in Beryl's care.

They appeared in the evening at the house and Petruska fed with the calf standing close behind. The elk arrived and nuzzled the calf. Petruska paid no attention, but when the bull arrived on the scene she chased him away. However the days of her dominance were nearly over. On 26 July Petruska arrived to feed alone. A little later Peterkin stalked up followed by the calf and Prissy. He came boldly up to the trough and began to feed. His horns, although still in velvet, were now too wide to permit her to feed with him. 'Ay ay ay,' she cried and surrendered the trough to him. From now on until he lost his horns in the spring Peterkin was boss and the family were together. Prissy was there too.

Peterkin rubbed off his velvet on 25 and 26 August. From then on his character changed. He was always on the lookout for another bull on whom to work off his repressions, but we did not fill the bill. On the whole he remained gentle, but sometimes he approached us stiff-legged, head slightly on one side, ears back, his eyes rather bloodshot and the white showing. As far as possible we ignored him although this was sometimes difficult when he paced just a moose's breath behind us. If he tried to bar the way as he used to the year before, we walked straight at him, telling him not to be so silly. Usually his nerve broke and he gave way but sometimes we had to threaten him, Beryl with her mattock and I with my broom handle. We had to maintain a dominance over him without allowing him to test how strong we really were. There were times when he was obviously upset, when he really did not seem to know what he was doing. Then it was best to avoid a confrontation, leaving him to tear a tree to pieces, like a bull horning the ground. At such moments our way would take us in a different direction, preferably one that put a few trees between us.

This may sound more dangerous than it is. Peterkin saw us or heard us every day of his life and in no way were we a threat to him. In fact we interest him because he will usually come and join us if we are doing anything in the sanctuary; but sometimes his desire for sex and battle is so strong that he is really confused. As long as we recognize this state and tact-fully avoid him we can get along all right.

His bad time was approaching. At the beginning of September he was jealous of any attention to the cow, crowding her at the feed trough and making what Beryl calls his 'nasty face' at us. Petruska also seemed to be reluctant to feed the calf although she still had plenty of milk. One day when Beryl was giving Petruska her bread, the calf dived in and had a good suck. Petruska protested with her 'ay, ay, ay,' complaint, but she was far too greedy to take any other avoiding action. Petruska came to the house more often now, sometimes out of breath as if she had been running and always complaining when she saw the bull coming.

In the middle of September we had Paul and Dona Anderson

over from Calgary. He is a tough sturdy professor of biology
keen on all outdoor things: canoeing, climbing and shooting
– shooting in the right way, that is over the hills and across the
valleys on foot in the early morning, after elk, moose or
whitetail. He has also contributed to a book, a collection of
articles and essays by himself and other authors, happily
named, 'The murder of the eco-system and the suicide of
man.' His speciality is mice. Dona, younger, always rather
breathless with excitement, a slim athletic figure, looked as if
she could keep up with him on ski or on the hill.

We walked down to the pond with them whence I returned
to the house to collect the truck, so that I might meet them at
the south-east gate and we could all drive on to the barn to
feed the horses. When I got to the gate I found Paul and Dona
fumbling with the combination lock.

'Clockwise fifteen, anti-clockwise thirty-seven, clockwise
twenty, that's what she said,' I heard him repeating.

I could detect a slight air of urgency. 'Where's Beryl?' I
asked.

'She's down the fence having a bit of trouble with the
moose. She wants you. She told us to come on and get you.
Clockwise fifteen, anti thirty-seven, clockwise twenty. I'm
sure that was it.' Suddenly the gate opened. The combination
lock always seems to have a will of its own. It is only when we
are almost defeated and decide to climb the fence that it relents
and opens.

I hurried down the fence line and found Beryl and Peterkin
walking together. 'He was most strange,' she said. 'I really
think that he's jealous of other people. He wouldn't let me
walk with them and herded me away.'

We decided that he just did not like us to be with strangers.

Towards the end of September both moose disappeared for
two or three days. We went out to look for them and as we

wandered towards the edge of the woods, Petruska burst out and hurried towards us. She gobbled up the bread that Beryl had brought for her, but she was nervous and had a truant look. It was not long before Peterkin arrived at a trot. He halted as soon as he saw us, and then commenced his stiff legged walk, stopping a few yards away to beat up an inoffensive tree.

'It's all right, old man,' I told him, 'you can have her,' and then Beryl and I withdrew so that Peterkin was between us and his cow. As soon as he found himself in this position he seemed to relax, but he would not let her follow us. Although on this occasion she submitted without trouble, on other occasions she made determined attempts to get past him, while he behaved like a top-class cutting horse, turning here and there on his hocks, anticipating her every movement and ably demonstrating, as I was taught many years ago at the Staff College, the advantage of interior lines of communication.

The whole of September Peterkin was in a bad way, in October he was beginning to simmer down, and by the end of November he was back to normal, that is to say he no longer seemed to be tormented by his sexual urge. All cows that are going to breed should have been bred by then and he was not in search of them or of other bulls to fight.

In the early part of the year his energy goes into the growing of his horns, in the fall to sex, and in the winter to the stern business of keeping alive and fit enough to tackle his enemies. During all the running and the pursuit of Petruska, the calf was there or somewhere not too far away, a puzzled shadow. As soon as Petruska was bred and Peterkin lost interest the calf stayed with Petruska. Sometimes all four were together, sometimes the bull went off on his own and Prissy seemed to be impartial in his choice but was always near someone.

9. Trumpeter Swans

When we decided to fence the drive we went back to the same firm that had put the game fence round the sanctuary and they sent one of the men who had worked on it before. We were pleased to see him as he had done a good job.

This time he had brought his brother. When they worked together they worked as if they were already late for a date, stopping only at times to hurry to the house in order to drink half a gallon of water. They were two stocky and hardy young men who, I felt, really should have been in a dory on the 'Banks' rather than in Alberta. They told us of their hunting in Newfoundland, and had great respect for moose. 'We've got to get the job done before he gets the velvet off his horns', they said and this became their objective.

We were putting the fence on a line out of sight of the drive where possible so they borrowed the Land-Rover in order to get through the bush. The new fence made an enclosure of about six acres which we later found useful when we wanted to pay particular attention to some animal. One of the brothers was soon back to ask for assistance. 'We'll never get this done,' he said, 'if you can't control the moose. He's got my brother on the roof of the truck and we can't do any work.'

We were not worried as his horns were still in velvet, but went up to the truck and persuaded Peterkin to follow us down to the pond. The Newfoundlanders set to with redoubled fury to make up for lost time. Peterkin rarely went to the pond by himself although he liked to swim there. We knew that once in the water he would quickly forget his interest in the new fence.

Garry arrived and soon after his coming the Newfoundlanders returned to say that the Land-Rover was stuck in a bog. We had a good rope in the garage and managed to haul them out with the Land-Rover's winch. At dinner that night while Beryl and I read our books Garry kept shaking his head and laughing.

'It's those Newfies,' he said. 'It takes a Newfie to get stuck like that in a Land-Rover.'

'You sound like a Newfoundlander talking about a French Canadian,' said Beryl.

Garry shook his head. 'They're all like that,' was his comment.

Next day he took the Land-Rover with a load of stones to stop up some holes under the fence. An hour later he was back on his feet, crestfallen. 'I've done it myself now,' he told us. So he had, but in a bigger and better way than the Newfoundlanders and there was no tree near to use as an anchor. We had to improvise one by driving fence stakes into the ground and lashing them together.

There were many places under the fence wire where a coyote could squeeze in, or Kochi, whom we did not want to wander, could squeeze out. One of our jobs was to fix chicken-wire to the fence bottom at the high places and then to secure it by filling the depression with boulders. There were no boulders in the sanctuary which had never been cultivated, so we brought them from the half section in the Land-Rover after picking them by hand. There are piles of stones along the old fence lines and sometimes in the middle of a field. The early settlers must have done a great deal of stone picking although the land in Grand Valley a mile away is comparatively free of them. The half section has a bountiful supply and if we were to cultivate it we would have to unearth many more. Probably the best way to use the land is to improve the grazing, and this we hope to do by harrowing and fertilizing, even by seeding and harrowing and by controlling the amount of stock and the time that they are on the grass. The day will come when the land has to be made more productive. If we can improve it in preparation for that day, this seems to be an adequate aim.

We have one field of about twenty acres which in the time of the previous owner had been covered with aspen. He had pushed the aspen down with a bulldozer into two long rows for burning, which extended the length of the field, but he had never burnt the rows. From the cleared portions of the field he had taken a crop of barley but it had not been sown to grass. It had been the most lamentable field, mostly bare earth, weeds and rose bushes with young aspen already sprouting along the edges of the rows of dead trunks. We hired a roto-tiller but after one or two passes the owner gave up on account of the stones. Beryl and I picked many stones off the field, and Sid Ball sowed oats to be cut green as a cover crop for grass on the part that had been tilled.

We got the oat hay all right but next year the field was hailed out before we took any hay and the cattle grazed it. Next year we harrowed the centre strip, between the rows of dead trees, harrowed and sowed the top strip lightly and left the bottom strip that had already been tilled and sown. Meanwhile we burnt many of the dead trees, taking care to preserve as far as possible the young trees on each side of the row, so that ultimately there would be two avenues of poplars running down the field which would provide shade for cattle.

When summer came the bottom strip had a good crop of hay, the centre strip which had never been sown but only harrowed had a great crop of grass and weeds, and the top strip which had been harrowed and lightly sown had an equal weight of hay but since it had been sown it was well mixed with clover. When the hay was cut and loaded and the cattle were turned in they would not leave the field. For the minimum expense it was a field again.

Although the top soil is very thin it's very fertile and if there is rain the seed seems to catch without a seed bed. On each side of the drive there were two bare ditches with all the soil removed. I scattered clover, creeping red fescue and timothy and in a year the banks were covered in spite of much of the seed having been washed away by a violent hail storm.

Beryl and I still enjoy stone picking. I expect an Albertan farmer would use a stone-picking machine, but we are out in wonderful country and, since we choose the day, in lovely weather. We pick a truck load at a time, intending to use the stones later. As I work I think of the stone walls that I have ridden over in Durham, the long stone walls on the Yorkshire moors, the walls in Ireland and the walls in Spain. Often huge stone walls picked off such tiny areas. How lucky we are to have not only so fertile a land, but one with so much grass and so few stones. Picking them seems to be an ancient and honourable occupation, a historical task and good exercise into the bargain. A load a day should keep the doctor away, or since doctors don't come these days, should keep us away from the doctor.

Beryl's object was to make the place a sanctuary for threatened wild life but so far we had only got individual animals who were individually threatened. Trumpeter swans are now no longer threatened but their breeding places east of the Rockies which used to be right across the prairie are now limited to Grande Prairie, with a few birds at Delta, Cypress Hills, Calgary Zoo and at Archie Hogg's farm near High River. West of the Rockies there are considerable flocks breeding and migrating but it has not been established that these are the same type of bird as those east of the Rockies. The trumpeters at Lonesome Lake, west of the Rockies in B.C., have become hippies, and when a large flock arrives from the north it stays there for a government hand-out of grain. So far they have resisted all attempts to persuade them to continue their migration further.

We were invited to a trumpeter swan conference at Grande Prairie three hundred and fifty miles north-west of Edmonton. We drove through miles and miles of forest which gave us some idea of the huge empty land, to a bleak town plunged in winter, although it was still only September, and to an hotel of uncompromising architecture, as bleak as the surrounding town; but like Canadians, its rough exterior had a warm heart within.

I have often thought that people particularly interested in some animal are apt to grow like the animal themselves. I have seen beekeepers who looked like bees, with mandible mouths, eyes that peer through lenses, and antennae that sprout above them; pigeon fanciers I have met have looked like pigeons, and everyone knows that horse lovers grow like horses. Beryl and I probably look already like moose. I cannot say, however, that any of the aficionados of the glorious trumpeter swan looked like swans. When I saw a group of them coming out of the hotel lift, I thought at first that it was the Russian hockey team, suddenly transported to Grande Prairie to pursue the life and death struggle that they were then engaged in with the Canadian team in Moscow.

The Americans were well represented at the conference and have had a great deal of success in the preservation of their birds. In their breeding areas they have special boats and films and men fully employed in looking after the swans. In Canada we seemed to have one man who, amongst many other duties, had managed to find time to organize the conference and to think of the swans. Perhaps the Americans, with more people to employ in swan care, more men technically qualified to head them, and more money to back them, would have liked to take over the organization of our swans. They could ring them and record them and transfer them by air if necessary, until a flight path was established. I thought that perhaps the swans ought to be consulted about this.

We saw slides of the American birds on their nests and went out to see the birds on the lake but they were far away. However one pair had nested in less conventional surroundings and raised two cygnets. By now the older birds had deserted them but the cygnets were doing well in their nesting place, on some water between a railway line and a barn. One of the Americans who had just written a treatise on the breeding habits of the trumpeter swan and had stressed their need for solitude was upset to find them happy in such suburban surroundings.

We came back stuffed full of information about trumpeters, having met many dedicated people. There were various difficulties ahead of us. First we had to make the pond suitable for trumpeters, then we had to provide islands for them to breed on, and there had to be suitable food. We had plenty of grass but they needed water-weed; bulrushes, sago pondweed, cattail and coon tail. Given all this we had the problem of how to get them migrating. Trumpeters are very territorially minded and the pond would only be big enough for one pair. If we got young ones with no old swan to lead them how would they migrate in winter? If we kept them a winter and fed them, why would they want to migrate next year? If we pinioned a pair who could not fly, how would they teach their young to migrate? I do not think that anyone knows the answer but we came away from the conference with the impression that the Fish and Wild Life Service would like to re-establish the old migration habits across the Prairie, perhaps by farming out breeding pairs. In such a situation it is possible that the territorial jealousy of the parents might drive the young away and they would once more fly south in search of open water. If the Fish and Wild Life Service did try to farm out breeding pairs we said we would like to help.

We had started making the islands the year before, using old motor tyres as a base, and covering them with brush topped by earth and sod. We started on four islands and must have put down hundreds of old tyres. One day when I came out of the pond I began to itch. An unbearable itch like an allergy, and I only got rid of it by getting into a hot bath. Beryl was sceptical when I told her. 'You're only imagining it,' she said, 'because someone warned us about slough itch.'

Next day she herself was in the water with very little on and came out, to my satisfaction, scarlet with irritation. This didn't stop her. She was in again next day wearing more clothes and was not bothered. I heard later that slough itch, which most Albertan boys know about, is supposed to be caused by a parasite brought in by the duck. Whether this is true, whether it only affects bare skin, or whether it is a combination of time and temperature, I am unable to say, but now, whenever I see duck preening themselves on the water, I wonder if they have the itch and they have my sympathy.

In order to make the islands we dragged the tyres, the brush and sods, out to the site on wooden rafts. The birch twigs were not a good enough foundation for the sods and the October storms washed most of the earth away. On one island the musk-rat took a hand and improved our work by weaving in reeds so that they had a regular house on the island, a useful seat later on when we were taking off our skates before meeting the moose who were waiting for us on the shore. Next summer grass was still growing on the waterlogged brush but the islands were not firm enough for nesting although the duck liked to sit on them. We decided that the foundation would have to be of stone. We had recovered an old dinghy from the coast, which used to belong to *Tzu Hang*, and with it transported hundreds of boulders to the island sites. These we covered with sods and sowed with grass. The grass grew well and we hoped that next year the duck would nest there. We might not have swans but at least the duck would benefit.

In order to have a big enough lake it had been necessary to raise the bank that contained it. Peter Heyes, a Yorkshire botanist who was studying at Calgary University, and some of his friends, had been largely instrumental in raising the dam. He is a great man with a wheelbarrow and a spade, although not without protest. He quoted to me an inscription that was graven on my porridge bowl as a child, 'If tha dost owt for nowt, do it for thasen.' Peter did a lot of work for nowt but it probably cleared his head for further studies. Bill Milne suggested that we were losing water from evaporation and that we should turf the dam. In the summer during which we started the islands we cut turf and put it on the dam. We took most of the turf from the piles that had been pushed aside by the bulldozer when it was clearing the fence line, and which were still green and growing. Some we picked off the road where they had been pushed to one side by Lin Fenton's grader. On this we sowed more seed and now the bank, which was once bare earth and stones as it had been left by the bulldozer that made it years ago, is covered with green grass.

Our next aim was to get some pond weed and for this we contacted Doctor Allen at Lethbridge Experimental Station. He told us that weed was being cleared from Lake Wabamun, west of Edmonton, and if we could meet him there he'd show us what we wanted and how to get it. We found him having a cup of coffee in a restaurant by the side of a large still lake that mirrored the grey skies above. There was a hint of snow in the air.

He told us that Calgary Power, from whom we get our electricity, were discharging the waste water from one of their stations into the lake and were accused of raising the temperature of the water so that the weed flourished. It seemed that the weed flourished in other lakes too that had no connections with Calgary Power, but the company, partly to soothe excited fishermen and water skiers, partly as an exercise in public relations, had undertaken to clear the weed from the lake or, if it could not be cleared, to keep it under control.

The weed was being mown by large waterborne machines that then ingested it. When their bellies were full they waddled off across the water like some prehistoric monster to a ramp, where they spewed the weed on to a moving track which carried it to a waiting lorry. Doctor Allen, an enthusiast if ever there was one, showed us the coon tail heads and told us to pluck them and then drop them in our pond.

We followed the lorry to a rubbish dump and there in the smell of decaying vegetable matter searched amongst the most recently dumped loads for the coon tail heads which we put into plastic bags. As we did so we felt like starvelings over a refuse bin. Presently Doctor Allen arrived. 'I've got to have a picture of you,' he said, opening his camera, 'I'm going to send this to Calgary Power to show them that at least there is someone who appreciates their weed. It will make a great public relations picture.'

We took a different road home and stopped at a village by another lake for a cup of coffee and a sandwich. The village is a holiday place and was now deserted so that it had a forlorn look, made doubly so by the dull day.

No one could fail to agree that Canada has its fair share of ugly villages and I often wonder why. Sometimes I think that it is because the beauty that surrounds us has made us feel it is sufficient, and we have failed to realize that our villages are an integral part of that beauty and that ugliness can destroy it. Yet no particular beauty surrounds a village in the flat prairie and one will be attractive and another dead and dull. Sometimes I think that it must be lack of planning and yet there are so many unplanned villages that are still beautiful. Then it must be lack of trees, lack of grass, and lack of flowers although individual householders usually do their best. Trees are the first essential. They bring birds, colour and a sense of peace. In the end I think that it must largely be blamed on the automobile, which causes the hideous signs at gas stations and the ugly 'drive-ins.' Even Cochrane with its heart of gold and its lovely setting, after a traveller has passed the bilious green of the concrete creamery and the chocolate notice board that welcomes the visitor from the west, aims a garishly painted red and white 'drive-in' like an Indian arrow at his heart.

At least the notice board is not as bad as the one that used to be outside Ripon in Yorkshire. 'Welcome to lovely Ripon,' it said. 'Stay a while and enjoy her ancient charms.' That always seemed to me to be an invitation to meet an old tart.

We found an exceptionally dirty and unattractive coffee shop but it had the best bacon sandwiches I had ever tasted. When I went to pay the bill a dark-skinned young man, his head resting on his hand on the counter, was doodling on the bill slips. 'I love love,' he had written and the rest was in Arabic.

I gave him the Arabic greeting, which is almost the only Arabic that I know. He jumped up and looked at me wide eyed.

'Where do you come from,' I asked him in English.

'From Beirut,' he said.

'We know Beirut, we've been there,' said Beryl as we started to leave.

'Come back,' he cried. 'More coffee. I give you more coffee. More sandwich.'

We spoke a little with him and then left. He came out to the car saying, 'Stay, stay. I give you more coffee,' but we had to go. We left him wringing his hands.

Peterkin and Prissy try their strength

A hot day!

Peterkin helps with the bonfire

truska and the twins

Kochi and Dilly

Prissy

Peterkin

10. Peterkin and the Camera Crew

Everyone is relieved when Peterkin's rut cools off, particularly Petruska who is left alone to go her own way. When the leaves are gone, by the end of October, Peterkin is himself again. He still thinks perhaps of lost opportunities: the sound of a breaking stick brings him out of the trees, he moons through the fence at distant cattle, and if a cow moose appeared that had not been bred he would still be able to serve her. But the embers are cooling and soon he will be thinking of keeping himself warm and fit, able to run and fight the wolves if they should pursue him.

That year he first showed that he was cooling off on 8 October. Beryl and I walked down to the pond to feed the duck. The track that a year before had been little more than wheel marks had turned into a grassy road. About twenty teal sprang out of the water as we came near, but they were old friends and settled again without traversing its full length. A few mallard left, already in winter plumage. They circled at some distance but came back over our heads in a lovely rush and swirled to land again before we had gone.

Suddenly we saw Peterkin close behind us. Although all the ground between us and the woods was virtually open we had not noticed him till then. He has this habit of materializing. At this time we do not want to have a confrontation with him. He is too big and strong and quick to rouse. The secret is to leave him guessing and to avoid disputing ground with him. He was a fine sight with his dark coat shining, but looking a little on the light side because of his restless rut. His horns this year had a thirty-one inch spread and the down-turned tines that he had as a yearling were ten inches long. They interfered when he turned his head to lick his flank. To our relief his ears were forward and he had a pleasant questioning look.

'Hello Peterkin, old boy,' I said, 'are you coming for a walk?' We kept in front of him, walking slowly round the pond, so that it did not look as if we were confronting him. He followed us peaceably, sometimes stopping to pull at a bush and then catching up again, all the way to the house. We get a great thrill out of going for a walk like this with a moose.

A few days later Peterkin was banging at the garage door. Beryl opened it and scolded him. He kept his ears forward, a surprised look on his face, then turned round and disappeared. Soon he was back again with Petruska. One cannot help thinking of moose as communicating with each other. We suspected he had said 'You have a try. She's mad about something.' Beryl flew to the door when she heard him knock again and wrenched it open. Peterkin had already backed off and instead she found gentle Petruska licking her lips while Peterkin stood back expectantly. Completely defeated, Beryl gave them both bread.

Much of Peterkin's time was spent in mock and sometimes not so mock battles with Prissy, whose sharp single spikes now twenty inches long, looked horribly dangerous. On account of Peterkin's horns growing sideways before they branched, and Prissy's straight upwards with only a slight curve, Peterkin's eyes seemed to be in danger when they attempted to lock their horns for a pushing match. In this daily combat they groped for each other like two wrestlers and when Peterkin finally felt that he had a hold on Prissy's horns he'd shove him steadily backwards while Prissy made his sharp complaining whistle.

The elk later learnt to disengage and, being very swift in his movements, would whip around to a flank, while Peterkin adjusted himself all too slowly for an attack in a new direction. Fortunately it never came home in time and the slow process of groping for each other's horns would start again.

One day when Beryl and I had been down to the pond Prissy joined us on our way back. He appeared excited, holding his head high and picking up a foreleg. I felt that he was trying the effect of a challenge on us and chased him away, whereat he put his head back and galloped off. It is easy to see why elk have such prominent eyes: since they have to put their heads right back in order to avoid getting their antlers caught up in the trees, they could not possibly see where they were going if they hadn't. Presently Prissy came running back at a high stepping trot still with his head back. When he got near us he put it down and started to cut right and left over the grass, like some movie star in a sabre battle. He was so quick with his cut and thrust at an imaginary opponent that we decided he would have to have his horns removed before he did some damage to Peterkin.

We telephoned Dick Robinson who happened to be home and not filming in Arizona or Utah. He came the same afternoon armed with a capture gun which fired a tranquillizing dart for a distance of about thirty yards at the outside. The gun was fitted with a telescopic sight; it was somehow typical of

Dick's character that he should have an excellent telescopic sight on a gun that only fired thirty yards. As usual he was dressed in tasselled buckskin and smoking his clay pipe.

We found Prissy by himself resting quietly in a dry marsh, the yellow marsh grass standing tall around him and a circle of willow bushes completing his seclusion. He stood up when we disturbed him. Dick, who had already loaded his piece, walked round him to get an easy, almost point-blank, shot into his buttock. Prissy flinched and moved a few paces as he received the dart, but then began to browse on the willows.

'He'll go down in a few minutes,' said Dick. 'Plenty of time. But when he is down we just have to see that he's sitting naturally with his head up. If he goes right down he may choke on his cud.' Dick lit his pipe while I handed the saw to Beryl and prepared to support Prissy in a natural position. We waited for about ten minutes while Prissy, quite unaware of our bad intentions, continued to browse on the willow twigs. Then, seeing us do nothing, he prepared to resume the siesta we had disturbed.

'Now he's going down,' said Dick.

Prissy settled himself comfortably and then looked towards us. He was alert and interested but not prepared to sacrifice his rest if we had nothing more to offer. He looked tranquil enough but not as if he were under the influence of drugs.

'Is it working?' asked Beryl, voicing the doubt that was now beginning to assail all three of us.

'No,' said Dick. 'That's funny. I don't think it is.' He walked towards him and Prissy immediately got to his feet looking perfectly normal, looking in fact as if he were saying, 'What are we going to do now?'

Dick decided to try another shot and positioned himself

again. Prissy could not have been more accommodating to a blind man but at the second shot he trotted off, pausing only to stamp his leg as if he had been stung by a hornet. He did not go far and, if anything, appeared more lively than after the first shot. We watched him for about fifteen minutes, then he wandered off in search of the moose.

'That stuff can't be any good,' said Dick. 'I'll get some more and try again another time.'

It was some weeks before he returned and although Peterkin and Prissy had been in constant combat, the clash of their horns and Prissy's shrill whistles sounding at any time of the day and even on moonlit nights from the woods around us, the only damage that had been incurred was a small puncture wound in the centre of Peterkin's forehead.

This time Prissy was even more accommodating and allowed Dick to shoot him from the doors of the living room. After the shot he soon appeared sleepy and began to sag. He lay down normally with his head up. We went out and while I sat astride him to keep his head up, the others sawed off his horns with a tenon-saw. There was a pinkish tinge at the centre of the bone at the butt. Prissy continued to lie there for half an hour, rubbing his chin from time to time in the snow, as if he were having pleasant dreams of green pastures and delicate hinds. When he got up he looked unsteady but not in the least distressed. He walked away as if still overcome with a desire for sleep. Next morning he was back, apparently unaware that his horns were gone, although he was obviously bothered by distance and timing when he confronted Peterkin. At no time, either at the first attempt or after the second, did he appear to associate us with the pricks of the dart, the slight sound of the gun, or his subsequent experiences.

At the end of October Peterkin came through the door at the front of the house leading into the garage. Its width is thirty-two inches but as it will not open right back on its hinges this is reduced to thirty-one inches. Peterkin's spread was exactly thirty-one inches, but as he was unable to centre himself so exactly as to come in directly, he had to tilt his head sideways. Although he was still in rut he was as gentle as could be. Both cars were in the garage, but we did not want to scare him by starting one up and backing it out so that he could depart by the sliding doors; instead we had to persuade him out of the door by which he had entered, and without alarming or angering him for he might easily remove a door post or the furnaces and air ducts. Beryl went outside with a piece of bread.

'Come on Peterkin,' she said, 'tilt your head. Gently now. Tilt your head.'

As she said this she kept tilting her head sideways. Peterkin gazed at her solemnly and presently tilted his head and came out.

It was just as well that he was cooling off, for a few days later Dick Robinson arrived with cameras and sound equipment for his filming. We had had a fresh fall of snow and it was a brilliant cold day, with musk-rat sitting on thin ice on the pond and diving through holes into the water below. Dick was as usual dressed as a trapper in preparation for his next film about an old character known as Grizzly Adams. Dick lives so much in the character of the people that he is representing in the films that when one day I came into the house and found him lying on the sofa in a beaver hat, smoking his clay pipe, and not bothering to get up, I had to remind myself that he thought he was Grizzly Adams. This time he had brought his lovely English wife, and as I looked at him in his tasselled buckskins, his hair and beard dyed white, and smoking his old clay I could not help wondering how the old devil had won her.

As in most things to do with films there seemed to be an army of people.

'But we can't all go,' Beryl protested.

'No,' Dick explained. 'If you take the screen, Miles, there are no wires attached and we can do sound recording from anywhere. From upstairs if you like, but you bring the screen along and take care of it as it's a valuable bit of equipment. Beryl, you come along too, and then there will be two or three of us with the cameras. That's all.'

Pat Robinson and the sound people went upstairs while we went off to the east. Beryl called and presently Peterkin appeared and allowed Dick to do some filming. It didn't go on for long, as Petruska arrived and turned out to be much more of a problem than Peterkin. She regarded the invasion with hostility and seeing the large screen that I was carrying, a shrouded bowl of aluminium or some such material, parts of it shining in the sun, she put back her ears and dashed at me. Beryl tried to intervene but Petruska brushed her aside. As she struck at me with a straight but fortunately inaccurate foreleg I crowned her with the only weapon that I had, the sound screen, which then flew out of my hands and fell at her feet. She reared up and struck down, whether at me or the screen I cannot say. I was already fleeing with surprising speed to take shelter behind Dick who was at least armed with the camera tripod. I felt as I imagine a virgin might, suddenly assaulted by someone that she had trusted and loved. In a moment the excitement was over. Beryl recovered the screen and, holding it in front of her so that it would not upset Petruska, made off for the house, Petruska followed already licking her lips in the anticipation of food.

The attempt at the collection of moose noises ended and we returned to the house, wary and scattered, like a patrol that has been ambushed.

'Did you get anything?' Beryl asked the sound man.

'Not exactly moose noises,' he replied, 'but I got shouts of "Look out, here she comes," and then heavy breathing.'

'We couldn't see what was happening,' said Pat, 'but it sounded awful.'

'It was awful,' I said, still rather out of breath and ruffled.

A few days later Dick was on the phone again. 'I'm bringing over a couple of wolves,' he told us, 'to get a picture of the moose's reactions when he meets them. I'm just starting off now.'

Almost at the same time some friends arrived for lunch from a ranch further west of us on the edge of the forest reserve. We told them that they would be able to see the moose and his meeting with the wolves.

'That will be interesting,' said the rancher, 'we're losing so many calves to wolves now.'

Ranchers are able to lease large areas of forest land at low cost from the government, for grazing their cattle during the summer, as soon as the calves are ready to leave the home pastures. These lands are usually unfenced, the cattle being confined by natural boundaries. Some may stray, some may fall and injure themselves, some may be porcupined, some may die from eating what they shouldn't, and some may be eaten by marauders. It is impossible to keep a close watch on them, but when the cattle are brought out and some are missing, it's the wolves that get the blame. Wolves are protected and this is probably the main complaint, but show me the rancher who would abide by the law if he were losing cattle, saw a wolf, and had a gun handy.

Dick arrived as usual with a regular troop and a small convoy of cars. There was someone to help Dick with his cameras, two wolf handlers, a pair of wolves, and an elderly and prosperous looking man and his wife, whom we understood to be some of Dick's backers in his next venture. He was wearing the sort of checked shirt that prosperous looking men wear for the Canadian woods under Brooks Bros sportswear, a deer-stalker cap, and was carrying a movie camera. Whether to impress his friends or as a result of Petruska's last effort, Dick had another man with him carrying a rifle.

'Good heavens, Dick, whatever is that for?' asked Beryl. 'I hope there's not going to be any shooting.'

'Better a dead moose than a dead man,' said Dick dramatic-ally. He had never taken such precautions before. I could see from Beryl's face that she thought he had got it all wrong. We set off again after sending any unnecessary persons upstairs, but were still lumbered with Dick's friend and his wife for whom I felt vaguely responsible, in spite of warning them that they came at their own risk, a statement that made me feel excessively pompous and stupid.

Peterkin took his time about making an appearance. I knocked a tree with a stick, a noise that always brings him along since he thinks it's another moose invading his territory. Presently he appeared in the distance, looking like some haughty dictator showing himself on a balcony to take the plaudits of the mob. Seeing a strange group of people, he began, after a suitable pause, to tack towards us, first this way and then the other in order that he might fully sample the wind that was bringing our scent to him. He continued his advance slowly and impressively, with his head held high. Dick was busy filming. Everyone was tense with excitement and the two wolves, perhaps a year and a half old and not quite to their full maturity, strained at the leash.

'All right,' said Dick, 'let them go.'

The two wolves lolloped playfully towards Peterkin, ears pricked and tails waving. We had had another fall of snow and it shone brilliant and unmarked in the sun. The sky was blue

above, the trees still and bare. Peterkin watched the approaching wolves and then suddenly turned and fled. Beryl and I felt
most embarrassed. We had told such tales of Peterkin and now
he had let us down.

'Oh dear. I'm afraid he's not a brave moose,' Beryl said
and looked at me in dismay.

As he ran, however, his moose mind was at work. No one
had told him, but suddenly he realized that moose didn't do
this – not for two wolves. He turned round and then came
back towards them. They watched his approach and as he got
near ran at him again, one feinting in front and one behind.
Here was a new Peterkin. He charged the one in front head
down but using his forefeet to strike rather than his horns.
The surprised wolf leapt to one side and as Peterkin passed he
lashed out with a hind leg. Beryl and I had never seen him
move like this. He whirled round in a brilliant flurry of snow
and charged again, striking with both feet together. To Peterkin this was all desperately serious, but the wolves seemed to
be playing. They appeared almost disinterested, taking it in
turns to bait him and sometimes casually sniffing at a bush in
a momentary break.

During all this time Peterkin's mane stood erect from poll to
tail making him an awesome sight, but it had little effect on
the wolves. From time to time he gave an angry cough quite
different from the gentle sound with which he was accustomed
to announce his presence to us in the woods. Finally he was
too quick for one of the wolves and sent it flying, whereupon
they both loped off in the direction of the owls.

'Oh dear,' cried Beryl, 'they're after the owls now,' and she
started to flounder through the snow to their rescue. 'You bad
wolf,' she cried to one which then came towards her, and
fawned like a dog on the ground in front of her. The handler
who had been blowing an instrument which made a strange

noise like a duck lure arrived and the two wolves, tongues lolling happily from their wide mouths, were soon leashed and in their truck again.

It had been a most successful show in the sunlight and amidst the flying snow although a dark fir tree had not made the best background for the action. When we got upstairs the rancher's wife said to us, 'I've never seen such wolves. They aren't a patch on our wolves. You should see ours.'

The end of the year can be lovely with hard frost and bright sun. We look forward to it because of the skating on the pond. One morning Bill and Lorraine Milne came to skate, both of them as at home on the ice as they are on their feet or on skis. In order that the moose should not interfere, we put Bill's car in the garage and our own in the drive, then let the moose through into the drive. Peterkin had not been behind the house for some time and started a thorough investigation. When we got back from our skating we discovered him with a large roll of seven foot wire on his head. The same wire that the game fence is made of, a particularly heavy gauge that cannot be bent with the hands. Peterkin had his horns firmly enmeshed at one end of the roll so that as he walked, about five feet of the roll stuck out parallel with the ground.

In one corner of the downstairs living room there is a workshop with two benches and the wall covered in tools. The tools are rarely where they are supposed to be and never where they were last seen, so we could not find the wirecutters. I tried to free the horn by hand but could not bend the wire. Peterkin who seemed to tower over me walked steadily forward in a circle while I pushed and pulled, Beryl tried to soothe him, while Lorraine hunted for the wirecutters. Presently she found them and I was able to set him free.

His strength is surprising. I had made some garden chairs

which we had put on the stones in front of the house. They are
rather special chairs since the bases are made of two trimmed
ends of the supporting beams of the house. They are fourteen
by eight inches by two feet. On this husky base a seat and
back of two by fours is fixed. Their disadvantage is that it
takes two people to move them. Beryl and I returned one
evening from Calgary after the time that the moose are usually
fed. Peterkin had climbed up on the terrace in his impatience
and removed a chair. We found him down by the willows with
a chair on his head, wearing it like a hat. No sooner had I
seen him than he got tired of his burden and tossed it off.
Then he horned it, removing some of the two by fours. They
were easily nailed back, but it is just as well to have husky
chairs when there are moose around.

The bulldozer, when clearing the fence line, had pushed the
trees to one side. I was cutting the trunks into logs for the
fire when Peterkin arrived. He stood over me, adopting his
overseer attitude, as if criticizing my handling of the power
saw. Sometimes he wandered off a few yards to try what he
could do on a tree that was still standing, but soon came back
to stand just in front of the saw as I was cutting. We were only
a few yards from the fence with the road just beyond. A big
car drove past and then I heard it slide to a sudden stop as the
brakes went on. It backed up and stopped opposite us. A
small man wearing a large western hat got out and crossed the
road. He took hold of the fence wires and peered through so
that his face was framed in one of the squares. Since I already
had one useless onlooker to whom I was paying no attention
I paid no attention to this one.

'Well I'll be gol durned,' he said.

I had never heard anyone say this before and supposed that
he was an American. I went on cutting another log and when
the sound of the saw had stopped, heard him say again, 'Well

I'll be gol durned.' Peterkin stood over me as before apparently, taking an interest in the selection of the next log. I was aware of the wire-framed eyes staring at me, but did not look at them. After the log was cut Peterkin and I moved over to the next tree. I heard a last 'gol durned' and then a door slammed and the car drove away. I wondered what tale he would tell when he got home or whether he'd keep silent.

When we are up by the road fence cars often stop to ask some question. Once in the 'hunting' season a car stopped and a big man in a red coat and red hat got out. 'Are you all posted here?' he asked. One of the unpleasant things about life in the Canadian country, particularly if living within fifty miles of a town, is that it is necessary to put 'No Trespassing' notices at each corner of a property if you want to keep hunters away.

'Yes,' said Beryl, 'what do you want to shoot?'

'Anything,' he replied, 'anything.'

'Not the moose,' we protested.

We have been continually warned about the likelihood of losing our moose during the moose-hunting season; so far we haven't been much bothered, though when we came here, we had at least thirty sharp-tailed grouse, some ruffed grouse and two coveys of partridges, sometimes on our property and sometimes on our neighbours, and three years later they had disappeared all but one or two grouse. In Canada one can drive for hundreds of miles and never see any game other than geese and wild duck. Fortunately the migrant duck and geese seem well able to look after themselves, but the upland game, the partridges and pheasants which are imported, and the grouse which are native to the country, are fast disappearing. Sometimes I think that we will end up like the Mediterranean lands with everyone out with shotguns for a day's sport after sparrows and starlings. Older people here remember being able to take their guns and get a couple of grouse in half an hour, but there is little hope of doing that now. The spread of civilization, the use of pesticides, and modern farming have taken their toll. One reason may be the spraying of the road edges from a vehicle, although I am told that herbicides have no ill effects on birds. Since I have been here I have not used my gun, partly because as I get older I have no longer a taste for it, and partly because there no longer enough game to warrant it.

The wild animals we could well do without are the porcupines – both the moose and the elk and one of my horses have suffered from them – yet they only want to be allowed to go their own peaceful and prickly way. Beryl and I and Garry were walking through the woods on the way to a bonfire when we saw something moving in the brush. It was moving faster than I had seen any porcupines move and at first I thought it was a badger, but it turned out to be a large porcupine in search of a suitable tree. It climbed up a fir tree, but there was another tree close to it, so I suggested to Garry that we might catch it if he climbed the second tree and pushed the porcupine out with a broomstick.

Beryl went off with Garry to bring a large dustbin, a long-handled spade and a long pole. I stayed to watch the porcupine. He climbed high but not high enough and he did not realize his mistake until Garry was level with him. If he had started to climb again he would soon have been out of reach but Garry was able to poke him. He turned his tail to Garry so that he was facing outwards and couldn't climb. Presently Garry was able to dislodge him. Beryl and I were waiting below and just as the porcupine's grip loosened Peterkin and Prissy appeared. The dog was already there.

'Look out,' cried Garry, 'here he comes.'

The porcupine rolled off a branch, fell and grasped at

another, fell again and so from branch to branch until it landed with a thump on the ground. Peterkin and Prissy had both suffered from porcupines but they had never seen one fall from the skies. It was too much for them and they both galloped off. Fortunately the dog kept her distance, and while I tried to head the porcupine off with the spade, Beryl endeavoured to put the dustbin over it. It was still very active but eventually she succeeded and banged the dustbin like a giant dice box over a rolling dice. We then slid the dustbin lid under the bin and up-ended it, tying the lid down to the handles with baler twine. We took the porcupine about seven miles away in the truck and turned him out in some trees. When he was first shaken out he scrambled back in, on his second expulsion he hurried off to the trees. Clio told us that porcupine are extremely stupid as their teeth grow right up to where their brain should be, and the need for gnawing has taken over that of intelligence. She also told us that they have strong homing instincts and can travel three miles in a night. She ought to know as she has a pet one which she can pick up and put on her shoulders, but I suspect that as far as the homing instincts are concerned she was pulling the parental leg.

11. An Oriental Chapter

I have always wanted a peacock, ever since while still at school I started reading Surtees and enjoyed the stories of Mr Jorrocks and his peacock Gabriel Junks. In India, where we went if possible to a jungle camp for Christmas, I loved peacocks for two reasons. First, because we used to shoot them for our Christmas dinner. This wasn't a very sporting affair since they betrayed their presence by flapping up into a tree to roost and we stalked them in their tree. Secondly, because of the way in which they sounded the alarm, a loud 'tunk', if they saw a prowling predator at night. There are few more thrilling things than being out at night in the jungle and hearing from the alarm calls of monkeys, deer and peafowl that a tiger is abroad. It is because of these circumstances and others, when I have seen peacocks wild and brilliant in the Indian sunlight, that they have become almost my favourite bird.

In our first winter friends from Edmonton rang up to say that they were on their way to Calgary and would look in to see us. They reminded us that they had met us on *Tzu Hang* a few years ago. 'I think I remember them,' said Beryl, but I could see that she was really scraping the bottom of the barrel and as far as I was concerned I had no clue who they were. A few hours later they arrived and as we went out to meet them, one look at our faces was sufficient for them to cry, 'You don't remember us.'

They stood momentarily disconsolate, each holding a sack in their hands. 'We've brought you a peacock and a peahen,' they said. If our welcome had lacked the immediate warmth that they had expected they could not have been disappointed by the delight that this news inspired.

'A peacock, a peacock,' I cried, as some treasure-seeker might shout at a cave mouth on finding a louis d'or at his feet. How could they have known how much I wanted one?

It was a black-shouldered peacock and his white hen that they had brought us. We called them Rama and Sita and put them in the barn, where they spent a miserably cold winter. They never ventured out except once when Kochi, galloping round the corner of the barn, came upon them suddenly in the sunshine at its entrance. Sita flew back to cover, but Rama, scared out of his wits, took off across the bright snow and landed in the top of a fir tree. In the afternoon Beryl climbed up to get him, but he flew off again and this time pitched in deep soft snow where he was held prisoner and I was able to catch him. They roosted on top of the hay bales and I fed them whenever I came to the horses, but they remained shy and would not come up to me. The barn is a cold place and I felt that they would have been much happier if they had braved the cold and come into the sunlight.

On a spring day they disappeared and it was a day or two

later that a farmer four miles away rang up to say that his children had captured a peacock. I brought Rama back and for the next two weeks he lived in the garage, going out only when it was sunny, and enjoying the warmth at night. Meanwhile our friend in Edmonton, hearing of our loss, gave us another hen. By then it was warmer and as soon as the pair seemed settled we turned them out. They roosted in the trees behind the house and wandered in the woods by day. Then Mrs Fox rang up to say that there was a white peahen feeding with her chickens. Sita had returned. The following evening Mrs Fox told us that she had shut the door of the fowl house on the peahen. We caught it by flashlight amongst a wild flurry of leghorns and feathers flying as thick as snow in a winter blizzard. Rama now had two hens and they soon seemed settled, although they wandered too far by day and sometimes we could hear Rama scream from deep in the woods.

One day Beryl and I came back from Calgary to find Kochi gone and Rama by himself round the house. I had a feeling of tragedy, and on the cut through the trees, where the power line comes in, I found two big puffs of white feathers. It looked to me as if someone had had two snaps at a peahen on the run. At first I blamed Kochi. She is a strange stand-offish dog and I wondered, although she does not like to come in the car, whether she might not have killed the peahens in a fit of pique at being deserted. Then I thought that perhaps a coyote had come while Kochi, taking advantage of our absence, had gone off to investigate the smell of some long dead calf, or to chew on an old leg she knew of, on the neighbouring ranch. Beryl insisted that some animal had come while Kochi was away. That she had been away was certain, since she only returned that evening, squeezing under the fence in one of her secret places. I searched everywhere and could find no trace of the peahens being dragged under the fence, nor any sign of their having been eaten. We put it down in the end to coyote or bobcat that had come while Kochi was away. Bobcat are about but very rarely seen.

We decided to build a peacock house for Rama for the winter. Peacock are extremely beautiful but their droppings smell strongly. They are not the birds for an indoor aviary or the garage. Garry and I made an octagonal house of eight foot plywood sheets on two by four frames with a conical roof. We covered the sides with the bark cuts from a saw-mill, horizontal and vertical on alternate sides, with a stable door entrance, so that the top might be left open for Rama's comings and goings. We gave him a good bed of straw and two perches. It had a pleasing rustic appearance; the only fault in design was that the radius was not quite large enough to accommodate Rama's full tail. By the time that he had grown it in the spring it had a slight curve. Rama appreciated his new home but he preferred the garage and whenever he heard its door go up he came running for warmer shelter.

The building of the peacock house was often delayed by the arrival of Peterkin, who cannot bear any form of activity to go on without him. If we were cutting fallen trees or building a bonfire, he had to be there. The sound of a hammer at any time of the day inevitably brought him to the scene. He was particularly jealous of our work on the peacock house because he was on the other side of the fence. We always had to be geared for other alternatives. When Peterkin started to horn the fence Garry and I took the truck and went off to stack wood for burning in the hay field. We might do half an hour's work before Peterkin arrived in the south-east corner, close to where we were working and started to try and push the gate down. Then we could go back to the peacock house.

If there was nothing else of interest he'd go up to the fence and stand about in the open till someone noticed him. Then he'd walk over to be admired. One morning we found a huge hay lorry stopped by the side of the road. A tall young man was over by the fence talking to Peterkin. 'I often stop to have a talk with him,' he said, 'he sure leans against that fence.'

'It's supposed to stop a charging animal, but I don't know how long it can withstand that pressure. We shouldn't really encourage him,' protested Beryl.

Now that Rama had a house of his own we got another peahen for him from the Zoo. She had only been with him four days when Petruska put her head in through the top of the stable door. We never saw that peahen again either, but the dogs found her remains in the spring. Perhaps she had tried to come back, but there was a heavy fall of snow soon after she disappeared so that she may have stayed in a tree and died of starvation. We were annoyed with Rama because he failed to look after his hens although he always took good care of himself. He became very tame during the following summer and was always displaying to the owls, the dogs, or to anyone who would pay him attention. Every gorgeous feather always seemed to be exactly in place and he stayed much closer to the house. He took to roosting on the dormer window of my bedroom and making his first scream at about four in the morning and his last at ten at night. In spite of this we had become very fond of him and were reconsidering the question of a wife.

Although Rama and we were pleased with the peacock house there seemed to be something missing, not only a peahen, but something else that would make the setting complete.

One day during our first winter Beryl went in to Calgary to see Lorraine Milne. The snow had not yet come but winter was near and the leaves had gone. She found Lorraine, slim as a willow wand, in her garden. She had a small circular fence that she was about to fill with earth and compost to make a flower bed next year. At the bottom of the proposed bed was a plaster Buddha about a foot and a half high.

'What are you doing with that Buddha?' Beryl asked.

'I'm going to bury him,' said Lorraine, 'I can't bear his expression.'

'But you can't bury a Buddha.'

'I wondered about that. But I thought that if I turned him into a flower bed it would be all right. Wouldn't it?'

'I don't think you should bury him,' said Beryl.

'I hate these things in gardens,' said Lorraine, 'but I saw him one week in Hudson's Bay at forty-five dollars and next week he'd been marked down to eight dollars. I couldn't resist the bargain. I felt sorry for him too.'

'I still don't think that you can just bury him. Would you like me to take him?'

'Would you?' asked Lorraine. 'I couldn't just dump him but I thought he might be all right under flowers. He has such a horrible expression. Please take him. It would be such a relief.'

When Beryl arrived home I too was struck by the malignity of the Buddha's expression. He was laughing, but it was a malicious laugh, as if he had just seen someone he didn't like slip on a stone bridge and fall into a lotus pond.

'What are we going to do with him?' I asked her.

'I thought that when we had finished the islands for the ducks, we could put him on one of them. Don't you think that would be appropriate? He's against shooting.'

We kept him in the garage and when Christmas came, and with it the grandchildren, we gave them a spray of gold paint to paint him with. Both Buddha and the children were soon covered in gold. It did not change his expression but it gave him a more expensive look. It was two years before the islands were finished and during that time Buddha rested in the garage. We then put him in the centre of the largest island which was covered with green grass. To fortify him against the winter he was given another coat of paint, this time of red. From the moment that we put him on the island it was shunned by the duck. Even when I put a decoy beside him the duck came no closer.

'I know what it is,' said Doug Buckle who comes to give us a hand when there is no fishing or shooting to distract him. 'The duck think that he is sitting in a hide.'

I looked at him through the field glasses from the upstairs living room. He did look as if he were sitting patiently in a hide. I almost expected to see a dog beside him.

'We'll have to move him,' I told Beryl, 'no duck will ever go near him.'

'I know what,' she said, 'let's put him on top of the peacock house.'

'And paint him gold again, like the Shwe Dagon Pagoda,' I suggested.

Doug and I brought Buddha from his island in the dinghy and transferred him to the top of the peacock house. We had had to shore him up with wood so that he looked comfortable and secure. Now he looks to the east and he has his peacock and the extraordinary thing is that his expression seems to have changed. Of course one can only see his face either from above, from my bedroom window, or from below. In either case he now seems to have a look of eager and merry anticipation, leaning forward slightly as if expecting something nice, perhaps the first ray of the morning sun when next it rises.

The professor who had stayed with us previously went off on a year's sabbatical leave. Before going he asked us if we would like to get in touch with a Japanese professor of microbiology who was coming to the university for a few months' post-graduate studies. 'You've been to Japan,' he said, 'and I'm sure that he'd appreciate it if you asked him out here. He may feel a little lost in Calgary. His name is Toshi Saito.'

Peterkin was just getting over his second rut when we remembered about Toshi Saito. I got his telephone number and rang him up. He seemed very pleased and excited when we asked him for a weekend and we arranged to pick him up at the address that he gave us. On the way to Calgary I found that I had forgotten to bring the address with me. 'It's either the corner of Twelfth Avenue and Seventeenth Street, or Seventeenth Avenue and Twelfth Street,' I said hopefully. Beryl said nothing. In the end a girl seeing us searching asked us into her flat so that we might telephone.

'But I'm not allowed to give you an address,' said the telephone operator. 'I can give you his number and you can ring him. We have a subscriber of that name.'

'But he's Japanese,' explained Beryl. 'We're late already. He won't be in his house. He'll be standing at a corner looking hopelessly this way and that.'

The thought of this pathetic figure broke down the operator's resistance and she gave us his address. As Beryl had expected we found him standing at the corner looking hopelessly this way and that. Before we left for the country he insisted that we should come back to his rooms and he gave us tea out of a small Japanese teapot with a handle like a file handle. We had bought a bottle of saki so that he might feel at home. His spoken English consisted largely of the words 'Yes, yes,' so that we wondered how he managed at the university, but we discovered that he could read English fluently. After a time, as we pressed more saki on him he became quite good with his 'No, nos,' too.

On Sunday morning we got up rather later than usual and by the time breakfast was ready we discovered that Toshi was missing. I guessed he was off with his camera. 'Did *you* warn him about the moose,' I asked Beryl, 'I didn't.' Neither had

she, so I set off into the woods to try and find him before he
ran into trouble with Peterkin. 'Toshi, Toshi,' I called, but
heard only the whisper of the wind in the trees and Kochi
barking at the last coyote as it and she turned towards their
resting places for the day. 'Toshi, Toshi,' I yelled but the only
answer was the scolding of a magpie. I wandered through the
silent trees calling, 'Toshi, Toshi,' It began to sound like a
lament and I pictured a small body lying crumpled beneath a
tree. Suddenly I heard a cough behind me and there was
Peterkin, tall and rather thin after his rut. He looked friendly
and his horns were clean. I went back to the house.

'No sign of him,' I called up to Beryl, 'but Peterkin was
there and seemed to be quiet.' At this moment to my relief I
saw Toshi, camera in hand, coming back down the drive.

'Where have you been?' I asked, 'didn't you hear me calling
you?'

'Yes, yes,' said Toshi brightly, 'I hear you calling Kochi long
time.'

Toshi soon returned to Japan, leaving Beryl his little teapot
out of which she drinks Chinese tea, holding the teapot by the
handle and drinking from the spout as she once saw it done
by an old Chinese, on a river boat bound for Chungking.

Shortly after Toshi's visit I heard from friends who had
sailed their yacht to Japan and were then in the yacht harbour
at Aburatsubo, enjoying the hospitality of our old friend
Fukutome. They told me that they had given our address to
three Japanese businessmen who were coming to Canada on a
publicity task for a new Japanese colour film; when they
arrived in Calgary they would get into touch with us.

Meanwhile two young and attractive English girls, finding
their way round the world as English girls are apt to do, from
friend to friend, had dropped in on us for a day or two. They
came from Gloucestershire and London and had been polished

and finished in the best tradition. I had picked them up sitting in blue jeans on the road side by the Ranch Grill in Cochrane after a night on the Greyhound bus. Caroline, Jim Kerfoot's eldest daughter, a microbiologist, was coming to lunch to meet them. She is small, overflowing with energy and full of fun, her manner sparkling and direct. We were looking forward to our lunch when suddenly the Japanese rang up. 'Could they come and see us?' they asked.

'Come to lunch,' Beryl replied.

When they arrived in a Toyota that they had hired they were delighted to find that we had three girls to meet them. It was exactly the sort of hospitality that a Japanese businessman would extend to three Canadian businessmen coming to Japan from Canada, although it is possible that the Japanese girls would be more in the line of professional hostesses. However our girls did their best. Their smiles flashed like beacons indiscriminately on our visitors and only froze occasionally while their eyes went glassy at too close camera confrontation. Their pictures were taken arm in arm with our guests and they were squeezed without complaint. Their photos probably feature in several advertisements for Sakura films. The Japanese were overwhelmed by our hospitality and the least sophisticated of the three kept shaking his head and repeating, 'Very cost, very cost.'

12. Hello my little Foxes

In the six months after a moose calf is born it grows tremendously, matching the virility of the short growing season that crams everything into four months, for it is only in the middle of May that the leaves appear and the middle of September that they begin to turn. By December a moose calf is nearly as big as its mother. After Peterkin's rut the calf was looking splendid, but Petruska was looking a little thin and was lame again. We supposed that it was from all the running that he gave her for it seems that unless a bull herds a cow until she is physically exhausted and has to submit to him no moose calves would be born.

In order to rest Petruska we put her in the few acres enclosed by the drive fences. The calf came too and as it was now in much closer contact with us, it soon became tame.

Petruska, who is always gentle with Beryl, sometimes objected to my being between her and the calf. She came at me several times with her ears back as if she meant to strike me. What with Peterkin trying to herd his cow away from me and Petruska trying to attack me to protect her calf, I began to think that the moose must regard me as some sort of maniac with tendencies towards perversion. For some time it had been obvious that the moose and the elk regarded me as male and Beryl as female. The two bulls, largely due to the tact with which we handled them, knew that I was the dominant bull. Petruska thought little of me but I was not prepared to be chased around by her. I found out that if I held out a piece of bread to her, arching myself like a coconut tree in a hurricane in order to be far enough away from her forward kick, her temper cooled. Bread was the key to Petruska's heart. Later I discovered that if I could get a hand on to her nose and tell her, with no great confidence that she would understand, not to be so stupid, her ears would come forward and she'd relax again.

The elk bull made a strange sound when he saw Beryl which he never made to me. He curled up his nose and made a long sucking noise which ended with a sound resembling the last of the bath water going down the plug. Beryl explained to two women who came to see the animals that he could tell the difference in sex. 'What,' one of them asked, 'even when you wear trousers?'

While Petruska was in the drive recovering from her lameness the local Fish and Wild Life Officer came to look at our pond. We were thinking of putting fish in to keep the water clean and to attract the heron which we had seen occasionally on its edge. He was a young and athletic fellow which was just as well, for Petruska tactlessly went for him and chased him round the peacock house. He went one way, but Petruska, as sharp as a needle, went the other way to meet him. Luckily the officer made the door first.

It seemed that Petruska was bred again, because the bull paid her little attention, although during their rest periods they usually came quietly together, sitting on either side of the fence. Soon Petruska seemed so well recovered that we put her and the calf back with the others.

When she was lame she was really lame and there was no pretence about it. She ignored it as far as possible and sympathy made it neither worse nor better. It was just as bad as it was. In this way she was rather like Beryl and Clio. I don't know whether Peterkin is more like me but the more sympathetic we are to him, the worse he gets.

One day he came to the feed trough very lame and I could not get a hand to his leg as he tended to horn me away. He put his bad foot over the wall at the feed place, as if he wanted us to inspect it, and at the same time rolled his eyes and put his ears back as if daring us to touch it. I suspected that the trouble was in the shoulder. The hair was roughed up as if Prissy had caught him a hard prod or possibly Petruska had struck him. He was very half-hearted when Prissy challenged him and made only a token resistance.

Next morning with a frost on the grass and willows and a low mist hanging about the pond I saw the moose family making their way in a very extended file towards the house. Peterkin was a long way behind but was moving quite well. The others were already at the feed by the time Peterkin got near. 'Oh you poor boy,' Beryl called to him, 'how are you feeling?'

I had watched him the whole way and from that moment he began to hobble as if he could only just bear to put his foot on the ground. The next morning he had recovered.

During all the time that we had had Kochi, she had never been bred. Her heats were not particularly regular; sometimes, like a wolf, only once a year. After her last heat she had had a phantom pregnancy. She prepared a couch for her accouchement under a bed in a room that we kept for visitors and, when turned out from this, under some bushes. Should anyone sit on the bed or walk past the bushes unaware of the approaching event that Kochi imagined, she rushed out snapping. She even produced milk for non-existent puppies and was in such a mixed up state that we decided that on the next heat we would take no special precautions.

She still looked a beautiful dog in spite of her nine years, and certainly not an old one. We were not particularly worried as the nearest dog was over a mile away: a Border collie whom his owner, Buck Drummond, credited with all kinds of intelligence, and who loved to ride on the topmost bale of the highest loaded hay truck, getting up there by his own extraordinary ability.

We had underestimated Kochi's need, as, when her heat approached, she went in search of a mate. She ignored the Boston bull terrier who also lived a little over a mile away, obviously regarding him as too small and noisy, she ignored Jim Kerfoot's neutered Dalmatian, whom she holds in disrespect, but introduced herself to the collie 'Chico'. She also introduced Chico to a hole in the fence that we had wired up but which she had torn down again. From then on he visited her regularly and even after all was over continued to pay calls to see that all was well. He was a very tatty looking collie with hairy ears, but he had a gay and endearing insouciance about him. One could not help feeling that he was a proper rake. One evening Buck Drummond rang up. He speaks very slowly and deliberately and is the manager of a neighbouring ranch. He is usually dressed as if for a trip to the Arctic although he makes a concession to the height of summer by wearing a western hat.

'Is that dog of mine, Chico, over at your place?' he asked.

Beryl looked out of the window and was able to tell him that Chico was there.

'Well just tell him that he's got to come home. Chico will understand.'

Beryl went out and told Chico that he was wanted at

home, but he paid no attention. She reported this to Buck.

'Oh well,' said Buck, 'we'll just have to let nature take its course.'

Nature took its course to the extent of five puppies which Kochi had, with no trouble, under the stairs since it was too cold to have puppies outside. Meanwhile Chico one day jumped off his master's truck and as he did so his hind leg slipped through a bracket on the side of the truck and he broke a bone in his hock. He was taken off to the vet who set the bone and put him in a cast. A week later I was driving down the road one night, when I saw by the light of the headlights a strange black shape hobbling along in the ditch. It turned out to be Chico on his way to see his bride. As a result of these excursions he had to go down to the vet to have the bone pinned and be re-splinted. After a few days, in spite of the most loving care, for everyone lost his heart to Chico, he escaped.

We were driving up Horseshoe Creek when I saw a boy that I knew standing over something black in the field. I stopped the car and called across to ask what he had got there.

'It's a dog,' he replied, 'I think he's got a broken leg. He must have been in a trap.' It turned out to be Chico at the end of the first stage of his sixteen mile journey home.

We kept two of Kochi's puppies, a black dog which we gave away later and a brindled bitch, the smallest of the litter. As she grew up she turned out to be in every way like her father. She loved to ride on the top of anything, loved to be with us, loved to go for walks; all quite different from the strange and cat-like independence of her mother. When she jumps she jumps a foot too high and then drops like a feather. She is very strong boned and active. She is like her mother only in that she always wants to be out. She has brought joy to Kochi's old age and by day they are always together. At night, while Kochis braving the coyotes, sometimes far from the house, her daughter remains in reserve by the front door. We called her Dil Khush – Happy Heart – and soon she became known as Dilly.

Dilly and Dally, as the black dog was then called, were always underfoot when the moose were around and daily we expected them to be trodden on or kicked. Once the calf did strike Dilly who let everyone know about it, but she has grown up quite unafraid of the moose and licks up the pellets from their bowl when they are feeding. The moose are fed on the wall of the terrace in rubber bowls which they never knock off. While they are feeding they work the bowl into a perilous position on the wall, but then shove it back with their noses. A horse would upset the bowl every time before it had finished and my horses, which feed in the same bowls on a counter, have to have a wooden edge made so that they cannot upset them.

At Christmas, when the country was once more under snow, subdued and still, the moose looked in good condition. Like the horses at the barn they spent more time near the house in anticipation of their feed time. Whatever the weather, in snow, or in the silence of severe frost, they never turned their backs to the wind, and always looked completely at home and comfortable, much more so than they did in the heat of the summer.

When browsing they did considerable damage to the young aspen, to my great annoyance, as they would break down a tree only to sample a twig or two. It was the untidiness of the broken trees that upset me rather than the thought that they would destroy all the young trees. Aspen grow from a spreading root system and this sort of pruning encourages new growth from the roots. There is also a great deal of willow on which they browse, plucking the tops of the bushes and doing no apparent damage. Two moose and their calves, provided that we get rid of the calves each year, are probably all that the 160 acres will sustain without damage or altering the character of the place. My fears that it will be transformed to a replica of Ypres Salient in the First World War are probably unfounded.

An old friend, Catherine Holmes, came up from the coast. I was away, but Beryl took her down for a walk to the pond and since the weather was so brilliant she suggested walking on round the fence line. Beryl is inclined to say that Petruska is always gentle with women, so she had no fears of trouble if they met the moose on their walk. Dilly who in a few months had wrapped herself in a rich brown coat with black stripes, and had tasselled ears like her father, accompanied them.

They had not gone far up the fence when Beryl saw Petruska following her. Peterkin, the calf, and the elk stayed by the frozen pond. As Petruska came up she put her ears back and ran at them. Beryl thought that she was after the dog and clutched at Dilly, but it was Catherine that she was objecting to. She tried to push past Beryl and strike at Catherine. Beryl dropped the dog and got her arms round Petruska's neck. 'Hurry up,' she called to Catherine, 'get over the fence but don't run and don't fall down.' Catherine made her way to the fence as quickly as she could but soon stepped into a large snow drift and found herself standing up to the waist in snow. She turned round and addressed Petruska, saying, 'It's all right Petruska. I haven't fallen down, I haven't fallen down.'

Beryl by now was hanging on to Petruska's bell and only delaying her advance. However, this was long enough for Catherine to extricate herself from the drift and climb to the top of the fence. Beryl then let go of Petruska, caught Dilly and passed her up to Catherine, who dropped her unceremoniously on the other side. Beryl then joined them without any further interference from Petruska.

At the end of February Petruska's calf was very lame. We

brought them both into the drive again and although the calf allowed us to feel her leg we could find nothing wrong except that at times there seemed to be a little heat in the foot. The temperature was below zero and diagnosis was difficult until one day I saw a little pus at the top of the heel, where the horn joins the flesh. She continued lame although with some improvement until a Chinook wind came and the ice and snow with which the bottom of her foot were coated disappeared. Then I saw the head of a nail sticking out of the sole. Beryl was able to pull it out with the pliers. It was a bent three inch nail. Somehow one does not expect a moose to get a nail puncture. The lameness soon disappeared and the slight separation between the horn and the heel closed up.

Beryl was away in March when Peterkin lost his horns. I particularly wanted to find them as we intended to put up his successive horns on a beam in the living room so that we could compare their growth.

Peterkin lost his horns on March 11th and 12th but Prissy did not lose what remained of his until the end of the month.

Anne and her daughter, Phillipa, who were looking after the house while Beryl was away, spotted the first horn in some bushes near the house, a day or two after he had shed them. A few days later I saw the other horn lying on the ice in the middle of the pond. The old ice had melted, but several sharp frosts had covered the pond with ice again. I could not imagine how the horn came to be resting on thin ice in the middle of the pond. Kochi or a coyote? It was far too big for them to have dragged it there. We went down and I threw a stone on to the ice. It went through. We had a roll of three hundred yards of baling twine. With Anne holding one end, I was able to walk round the pond till the twine stretched across the ice. We hooked it over the antler and then were able to drag it a short way towards the edge before it turned over and the twine slipped off. We tried again but soon the moose and the elk arrived and I had to escort Anne and Phillipa back to the house.

I could not bear to think of losing the antler if the ice melted, so soon started off to have another shot by myself. I tied one end of the twine to a bush and then went round the dam to try the same method again. I had barely started before the moose and the elk saw me and came running from the direction of the house. To my surprise they sploshed straight into the lake but without sinking more than a few inches as the old ice was still there under the new thin ice. They walked straight across to me breaking only the thin ice and must have been doing the same thing when Peterkin dropped his horn. I was able to walk in and collect it. Both Peterkin and Prissy became very excited on the way home as if protesting at the removal of the horn. I thought of threatening Peterkin with it as I had no other weapon but then decided that it would not have been in the best of taste.

We separated the calf from Petruska that month, keeping the calf in the drive. It had to go to the Zoo since they had given us its parents. It was now as tall as Petruska and very gentle. We were able to handle it and dreaded the awful betrayal that we were going to perpetrate when we boxed it and sent it off. The Zoo having lost their bull as a result of tranquillizing it when moving it from one enclosure to another were reluctant to tranquillize the calf. They lent us a trailer in which we fed it and then one day shut the door on it. Although accustomed to going in and backing out of the trailer it had never been confined before. Directly the calf found that it could not get out it was frightened and distressed. We fed it carrots and pellets and it snatched at them as I have seen a horse that has been staked, with its gut hanging out, pluck nervously at the grass. We could not help wondering by what right we con-

ned animals and though our two moose seem happy, the bull
usually and the cow always contented, our excuse is that they
were foundlings and would have died, but the thought of
what to do with a succession of calves worried and perplexed
s.

One thing that we could do with calves was to give them or
ell them to zoos and as moose are so hard to raise successfully
hey are of considerable value. On the other hand, having
aised a calf in the freedom of our land we are reluctant to let
hem go to a zoo where they are in a restricted area and have
ttle if any privacy and often no shade.

One day a letter arrived from the Misty Mountains Safari
Game Park in Montana. It had an attractive letterhead on
xpensive paper. 'We are starting a small safari game park
ere,' it read, 'and understand that you may have some moose
vailable. If so we should be interested in acquiring them.'

'That sounds just the thing,' said Beryl, 'you should write to
hem and say we will have a calf for sale but tell them that they
would have to be responsible for its transportation. It is
robably one of those big areas where cars drive through and
he animals live in natural conditions. Tell them that we are
nterested in what sort of conditions the moose will be living.
ou know what Americans are. When they say small it
robably means thousands of acres.'

'I'll write and ask what are their moose facilities,' I said.

We received no answer to the letter and some weeks later
ent down to the opening of the polar bear complex at the
algary Zoo. This was really the sort of place that we would
ke to send a polar bear cub if we had one. A country club for
olar bears, an Upper Canada college for cubs. Bill McKay,
usy with all the details of the opening ceremony, found time
 give us a moment.

'Do you know anything about the Misty Mountains Safari

Club in Montana?' Beryl asked. 'They would like to take
moose calf.'

'I don't know of it,' said Bill, 'but it's possibly one of thos
parks where Americans come to shoot so-called wild game. /
gun club.'

'I wonder what they thought of my letter asking wha
facilities they had for moose,' I said to Beryl later.

'As nutty as a fruit cake, I should think,' she replied.

We have had people come to the house and after seeing th
moose they have said that they would never want to ki
another one. I am not against hunting; in fact I think that youn
men should hunt, but they should do it the right way. The
should kill with compassion and they should put themselves o
as level terms as they can with the animal they are hunting
that is to say that they should find and kill him on their fee
I am against the telescopic sight, as in my opinion it induce
hunters to shoot at far longer ranges with greater risk o
wounding than the open sight. If a man has not got the ski
and endurance to get close enough to an animal to ensur
killing it over an open sight he should not be on the hill at al
nor should he be out if he cannot find it himself. If he has mad
so much money that he can hire helicopters and guides it show
a singular lack of maturity that he should wish to shoot at al

I have loved my shooting and would not think of denyin
the pleasure to others. But it must be done with humility; an
the glory is to the country, to the beauty of the early mornin
and the dusk, the whistling or the sudden whirr of wings; t
the breathless heights and the sound of a stone falling, or th
dark forest and a breaking twig. These are the things t
remember and give thanks for, and in order to have them th
game must be both hunted and preserved. But there are n
grounds for conceit in shooting game at long range, with
flat trajectory, high velocity rifle with telescopic sight, an

even with the use of a 'walkie talkie' between pairs of hunters.

On 30 April, a day of low cloud and fog, we saw eighteen big swans on the pond. They looked enormous after the duck and the Canada geese that sometimes pay us a visit, especially in this sort of weather. I thought that they might even be trumpeters on their way to their breeding place at Grande Prairie, but it is more likely that they were the whistlers who fly over on their migration. Through the telescope upstairs I could see no sign of the small yellow spot behind the bill which identifies a whistler, but they don't all have it and it is hard to see. Unless trumpeters and whistlers are seen together it is difficult to tell which is which, except by the noise they make. These came while we were away and left the same evening in unusual silence. We were so pleased to see them, so honoured by their presence. They looked so aloof and wild, such very superior birds that we felt almost in despair at their departure, as if we had failed in offering them adequate hospitality.

May arrived and once more the leaves burst forth, the flowers and the green grass appeared and Petruska disappeared to calve. It was ten days earlier than on the previous year and this year she showed that she was carrying a calf. I predicted twins but Beryl was not so sure. I left on a visit to England and when I telephoned Beryl from there she told me that I had been right. She found them within a day or two of their birth and this time the cow came up to her with her two little reddish brown calves close behind her, as if to show them with pride. The year before she had always hidden the calf before coming to see us. It was the nearest that Beryl has so far been able to get to them, although we may be able to tame them in winter. It is a strange thing that the calves should be nervous of people, when the mother has no fear of us at all. Petruska's last calf had been much tamer but was introduced to us perforce as she did not like to leave her mother. The twins found com-

panionship in each other and were much more self-sufficient
so that sometimes we did not see them for weeks. At five
months old they were already wearing proper little moose
coats, and only then began to approach the house with their
parents and to regard us with less suspicion.

While I was away Beryl heard from Mrs Vona Bates in
Colorado who said that she had two pairs of northern kit foxes
ready for her. Mrs Bates is a regular fox woman with whom we
had been in touch for some time. Her passion is for foxes. The
northern kit fox has been extinct in Canada for some time
although they still exist in Wyoming, Montana and Colorado.
They are on the endangered species list and Beryl was only
able to get them since they were already in captivity. As the
whole object of our sanctuary was to do something for endangered species Beryl was very excited at the idea of getting
two breeding pairs of these foxes. They were to be put in a
run that we had already started at the back of the house. Now
Beryl and Garry worked furiously, with Peter helping too, to
get the run and two kennels finished in time for the foxes.

Then she flew to Colorado to collect them. When I telephoned from England I asked how she was, knowing how
much work I'd dodged.

'I'm exhausted,' she said, 'and I've set fire to the house too.'

'Set the house on fire?'

'Yes. But we put it out again. Luckily Garry was here and
the garden hose was long enough.'

She sounded tired but as she has great powers of recovery
I did not worry. I gave her two days and then telephoned
again. 'Hello,' she said, in her usual cheerful voice, 'yes, I'm
fine. But isn't this getting rather expensive?'

When I got back the foxes were feeding out of her hand.
They were gay little things, floating around their big run so
lightly and quickly that they seemed to fly rather than to tread

the ground. They reminded me of dragonflies, so delicate and quick were their movements. When they chased each other in play, and sometimes in strife, through the culverts that we had buried for them and round the trees, their movements were so swift, their turns so sudden, that it was difficult for the eye to follow them. Kochi ignored them but Dilly liked to watch them through the wire and they followed her progress with little barks of interest. Sometimes the oldest fox had an eye to eye confrontation with her, accompanied on his part by hysterical screams. Whether this was partially play or whether he was threatening to tear her to pieces, I cannot say – he would certainly have found this difficult since she was now almost full grown and he was the size of a Siamese cat.

The northern kit fox has an alert look, amber eyes, a grey coat tinged with ginger, a gingery stomach, light brown legs and pricked ears. They have black marks on each side of their muzzle, a black patch near the base of the brush and a black tip. There are various kinds, but the northern kit fox has smaller ears than the desert ones. Perhaps he finds it easier to keep them warm.

The oldest fox had a broken foreleg which he got as a cub when a coyote caught him through the wire of his cage, before he came to us. The bone has never knit, so even today he is a three-legged fox although he uses his broken foot as he runs, flapping it down in a negligent way, as if he couldn't be bothered with it. Our vet longs to operate on him and splice the bone, but we will see first if he breeds again. Beryl called him Nelson because of his broken foreleg and the courage with which he confronts Dilly through the fence.

He and his mate Emma, who can be recognized by her paler eyes and rounder figure, had already had one litter before they came to us. Vona Bates, who has had such long experience with kit foxes, told us that the pairs become very attached to each other and that they probably mate for life. Her experience has been that if one of a pair dies the other is very reluctant to take a new mate. The other pair, Napoleon and Josephine, we cannot tell apart, nor does their behaviour give any clue as to which is male and which is female.

There is a nostalgic call that I now associate with this place. 'Hello my little foxes. Where are my little foxes?' it goes. I haven't to look out of the window to know that Beryl in her old working overalls, is approaching the foxes' run with a bowl of chicken necks in her hand, and that her little foxes, like the shadows of flying birds on the ground, are skipping silently across from their kennels to meet her at the gate.

13. Peterkin becomes a Film Star

One midsummer night, when the upstairs rooms were still warm from the sun which had smouldered down behind the Rockies, when the land outside was already cool and still and the peacock had long ceased his tramping on the roof, Beryl and I were both asleep. Presently the insistent and alarming clamour of the telephone awoke us.

Beryl was up before me and I could hear her hurrying through the big room to reach it before it stopped. 'Hello,' I heard her say, in her cool unruffled voice, although I knew that she was wondering wildly who could be ringing at this time of night.

'From where? From Juneau in Alaska. Yes we have. Well I

don't know whether she would let you do that. She's very protective you know and I don't know how she would behave with strangers. Well all right, I'll expect to hear from you then. We will be here anyway.'

'What was that?' I asked.

'Someone calling from Alaska,' she replied, 'he wants to bring an actor to film the calves.'

'What actor?'

'I don't know. He just kept talking about an actor.'

'Who was calling?'

'I didn't get his name. Chuck something or other. What a time to ring up. He'll be on his way down here in a day or two and will call us when he arrives.' She got into bed in a way which means that wars, earthquakes, or actors she is going to sleep.

Every evening, partly because she wanted to check on the cow and her calves, but chiefly because she hoped to get the calves tamer, Beryl took a bucket of feed and a short length of hosepipe and went in search of them. The length of hosepipe was to discourage the elk should he get too interested in the feed.

During these searches, if it was still hot and the flies were bothering her, Petruska and the calves would remain hidden. But sometimes she came alone, always announcing her arrival with a little cough. One can walk through the woods without seeing anything but the grey trunks and the green grass spotted with the yellows and blues of prairie flowers, through shoulder-high thickets of close growing young aspen, push one's way through willows, wade through marshy ponds thick with tall coarse grass, and see never a sign of a moose except the depressed grasses where they have lain, and then suddenly there would be this little cough and a moose close behind. More rarely the calves came too. Beryl was never able to ascertain what particular communication Petruska had with the calves to tell them that it was all right and that they could come out from their secret places. When they came they remained at a distance, two reddish brown high-stepping babes in the wood, big ears pricked, short noses testing new smells. Both were prone to sudden alarms and quick dashes to closer cover.

About a week after the telephone message we had another call to say that the photographer, Chuck Keene, had arrived at Kananaskis, thirty miles away. He would be along shortly, he told us, with a friend, but not the actor, and would like to get some shots of the calves. We were having our tea when I heard the dogs barking and looked out to find a veritable Ark Royal of a camper in the drive. As I approached it a man with close cropped hair and the figure of a Sumo wrestler stepped out. He held out a surprisingly small hand at the end of a pear shaped arm, enormous at the shoulder and strong in the fore-arm, so that the hand looked rather like the paper frill on the end of a large ham. 'I'm Chuck,' he said, 'and this is Dick,' introducing a smaller man who followed him out. 'Dick is a fixer. He can fix anything.' Not only did Dick turn out to be a fixer who was soon fixing a stove for Beryl, but also the Boswell to Chuck's Johnson.

'Come in,' I told them, 'we're just having some tea.'

My first impressions of Chuck were all wrong and they changed quickly. He had a figure like one of those toys that cannot be knocked down. He was short and the nearer to the ground the broader he got with a big stomach hanging over his belt. I don't think a charging bison could have knocked him down. I thought that he was too fat and that he talked too much for no sooner had he sat down to tea than he gave us a monologue on all the distinguished generals that he had met and interviewed. Yet he gave it in a self-deprecatory way. To begin with I regarded him with the deepest suspicion, but in fact all this was only his way of introducing himself to me. I had been a soldier so he wanted me to know that he wasn't just an ordinary person.

He told us that he was once a logger, and since he had little education the only way to get about the world as he wanted to was to get a movie camera and start taking pictures. His first pictures of Alaskan wildlife were accepted and he was given a job working for Walt Disney. Then he became a war photographer and had made seven trips to Vietnam. He must have been regarded as a bit of a Jonah by the helicopter pilots because a helicopter in which he was doing photography was brought down on three different occasions.

He had a smile which showed strong teeth and once he had finished his life story and the account of all his meetings with the great, we heard no more of it. He had a good sense of humour and enjoyed laughing at himself. His fun and friendliness were always bubbling over, in an enthusiasm which made him attractive, and his large body barely concealed in baggy grey flannels and a sweat shirt, was as hard as nails. 'You should see him go over the hills carrying that big tripod and camera. He can run for miles,' said Boswell.

After tea Beryl and Chuck went off in search of Petruska and her calves, she leading and Chuck following with his heavy tripod and camera over his shoulder, carrying it as easily as a city man carries his umbrella. They found them quite soon lying in a marshy wallow. Beryl planned to feed Petruska and then to step aside, so that Chuck could film her. Everything went splendidly until Beryl moved away, when Petruska became aware of Chuck for the first time and advanced towards him with her ears back. A moose's ears are expressive and restlessly lovely things, usually giving the impression of mild interest and tranquillity. When they put them back they lay them close down the neck, so that the tips are pointing to the ground. When a cow moose does this she looks like a cleaning woman who pins a cloth on her head, seizes a broom and sets about some unpleasant work with a look of determination to get it finished with quickly.

Chuck realized that he was the unpleasant bit of work that she wanted to get finished with and moved off at something between a fast shuffle and a run. When Petruska drives the bull away from her calves she will hunt him away, turning as quickly as he does, like a cutting horse and a calf, but with humans she seems to be satisfied with a token withdrawal. As soon as she was certain that Chuck was on the run she turned to Beryl for more feed. This was repeated several times but Chuck is nothing if not persistent and was rewarded by a good shot of the cow and her calves leaving the bog.

'I'd like to come again,' he told Beryl, 'the light is going now and I want to try with a bit of sunlight. Next time I'll leave the camera when I withdraw so that I won't waste time setting it up again. She won't touch it, will she?'

Beryl thought that she wouldn't.

When they got back to the house they seemed very pleased with themselves and, as I am particularly fond of Peterkin, I thought that Petruska was getting too much attention. 'You really ought to get some shots of Peterkin,' I told Chuck.

'I guess I've got plenty of good shots of bull moose,' he replied, 'and to tell you the truth, I don't think your Canadian moose can compare with the Alaskan.' As Peterkin at three years old was already nearly nineteen hands and his neck was filling to give him the strength to carry a fine rack which was now in velvet, I wondered what the Alaskan moose looked like.

A few days later we had another telephone call to say that

the Ark Royal was under weigh again and heading in our direction. 'It's no good coming before seven,' Beryl told Chuck, 'they really won't do anything before the flies have gone.'

Soon after eight, while the summer sun still gave plenty of light, they found the cow and her calves in an open place. The calves were shy and stayed away from the cow when she came up to Beryl, but Chuck was able to manoeuvre so that he could get some pictures. These were interrupted again by the aggressive behaviour of the cow. Chuck left his camera behind. She came up to it but only smelt it, before she turned back to seek more feed from Beryl.

'I thought I'd been crazy to leave the camera behind, once I'd got away,' said Chuck later. 'She might have done it some damage.'

'You couldn't do that with the bull,' Beryl told him, 'he'd have it over in no time; and speaking of bulls, here he is.'

Peterkin joined them on the way back to the house, stalking slowly beside them. Petruska was showing her ribs as feeding two calves was taking a lot out of her, but Peterkin, except for the fly sores just above his hocks, was looking splendid. His antlers had just about reached the limit of this year's growth and the velvet looked now as if it fitted close to the horn and would soon be dry enough for rubbing. His coat was black and oily and he was sleek and well covered. He was still gentle but as he walked beside Chuck he had his ears back, rolled his eyes and slobbered. In spite of this it seemed he was thinking more of the small hand-out of feed that he knew Beryl would give him, than of the stranger walking beside him. Chuck was suitably impressed.

'What do you think of him now?' I asked.

'I've never see a moose with a coat shining like that,' he

replied, 'and for a three-year-old he's tremendous. I think you have a champion.'

I may be biased, but I think it would be hard to find a better-looking moose, even in the wild and certainly in captivity. The reason is that he has adequate browse, room to wander, shade and privacy. More than any animal I know, a moose needs room. He is an animal of empty forests, of great vistas, of mountains, lakes and rivers. Although we cannot give them anything like the freedom of a moose in the wild state, ours seem to accept the restrictions of the sanctuary without yearning. Except for Peterkin's adventure in travel abroad it is all that they have ever known. It has the views of the mountains, which perhaps they don't appreciate, and the privacy of trees, and they look well and contented. The moose that we have seen in some game parks and zoos, restricted to a couple of acres of bare ground, seem by contrast to be unhappy and melancholy prisoners.

'I want to bring the actor when I come again,' said Chuck. 'I'd like to have some shots of him with the moose. I'll be in touch with you.'

The Ark Royal disappeared down our drive on its way to Prince Rupert, where the men would take ship to Juneau to celebrate the Fourth of July with their families in Alaska. Before leaving, Boswell told me that Chuck had bought a mountain in Alaska and was going to put up a ski lift. We next heard from him from Switzerland where he was looking at ski lifts; it seemed that only a few days later the telephone rang again. Chuck was in Banff with the actor and hoped to pay us another visit.

This time he had caught us in our baths. I lay still, hoping that Beryl would get out, but there was a determined silence from her bathroom. So I ran dripping to the telephone.

'Does the moose eat flapjacks?' he asked.

'He eats bread. He's never been tried on flapjacks. Why?'

Chuck began to laugh. 'I've written a little skit about him for this Mad Trapper thing we're doing,' he said in his deprecatory way. 'The Mad Trapper is cooking his flapjacks when the moose arrives and eats them out of his frying pan.' By this time he was laughing so much that there was a pause in the story.

'Wait a minute, I'll put you on to the moose woman,' I said, determined to make Beryl suffer too, but the conversation had already brought her, towel-clad, to the telephone.

'I've never tried him with flapjacks,' she said, 'I don't know how to make one. Perhaps we could put some bread in the frying pan and he'll eat that. There is so much feed these days that he isn't even keen on bread. I'll start feeding him out of a frying pan anyway,' she added brightly.

'I guess we'll fix something,' said Chuck.

When Peterkin came round that evening his empty bowl was standing on the wall in front of the house where the moose are fed. Beryl put the frying pan full of moose pellets beside it. Peterkin nibbled at the pellets and looked at Beryl. He then gave the empty bowl a push with his nose and looked back at her, ears forward and his eyes solemn and wondering. He was telling her as plainly as a moose can tell, 'Wrong bowl, you stupid.'

Ark Royal arrived a few days later. Chuck and Boswell were already out when I got to the camper and introduced me to Ford, the film director, a clean-shaven, grey-headed man with a gentle manner, dressed in blue jeans and a white singlet. His kindly aseptic look reminded me of a hospital orderly. Next out of the camper came Vic, a huge man who had once been a professional wrestler and had later coached Florence Chadwick for her Channel swim. He had straight black hair, cut in a bob at the base of his neck and a narrow black moustache. A merry wide-mouthed face but as he was already made up to look like an Indian halfbreed I could not place him. He was wearing jeans and a checked shirt.

'This is the bad man,' said Chuck, introducing him, 'the Mad Trapper is still inside.'

Shortly afterwards Mike, the Mad Trapper, appeared. He was even bigger than Vic and had also been a wrestler. The consecutive appearance of these huge men, both of whom dwarfed Chuck and looked as if they weighed a hundred pounds more than I did, made me feel as frail as a willow sapling. Mike had a broad furrowed face, the furrows emphasized by make up, under a strange round blue hat, like a short tarbush without the tassel. He was wearing an unbuttoned waistcoat over a checked shirt and heavy black serge trousers at least a foot too wide at the waist, although Mike lacked nothing there. The trousers must have been put on last as his scarlet braces which supported them were over the waistcoat. It was too early to expect the moose, so they all came upstairs for tea, prowling round like the three bears, although they could never have got into one bed unless it had been the great bed of Ware. In spite of their uncouth appearance or perhaps in strange contrast to it they had an elegance of movement, good manners and slow polite speech.

Beryl was soon talking to Mike about his past, and we discovered that, like Dick Robinson, they lived in the role that they were playing. We soon became half convinced that here was the Mad Trapper, and the halfbreed Indian who had hunted him and tried to betray him.

'Did you really kill the Mountie?' asked Beryl.

'But it wasn't my fault,' said the Trapper. 'They told me to open up my cabin door in the Queen's name and I said that I wasn't going to open up anything until I knew more about them. Then the young one got excited and said he'd shoot the

door down and before I could do anything he fired through
the door. Of course I fired back and I killed one and wounded
the other, but it was self-defence. At least that is what I call it.
I never meant to kill them.'

'And are you really after him,' asked Beryl, turning to Vic,
who was holding a small teacup in his large hand, and had
just been restrained in the nick of time from sitting on a small
nesting walnut table from Kashmir.

'Yes,' he said, 'I'm the baddy. They've offered a big reward
for catching the Trapper but he's a bad man to follow and I
don't know where he's holed out. However I know he has
some tame wolves and if I can find where they are, I think
they'll lead me to him.'

They talked on in their pleasant slow spoken way until it
was nearly seven and as there was still no sign of the moose they
decided to set up the Mad Trapper's camp, just below the
house and close to the wall where he was always fed, so that
they would be ready for his arrival.

'We'll shoot from an angle so that it will look just like wild
country,' explained Chuck, 'and if the elk comes we can shoot
him too, although the Mad Trapper wasn't really in elk
country. We want to show that he was good with animals and
the elk could be some place else, in earlier days perhaps, further
south.'

As if he had heard this suggestion the elk appeared in the
distance just as the camp was finished. He was still in velvet but
his horns were magnificently and symmetrically grown. He
came stalking slowly towards us, head high, alert and suspicious. Chuck got some splendid film of this wild creature
coming out of the woods, but he was suspicious of the
strangers, and would not come near the camp. Beryl enticed
him with his feed bowl, then put the bowl behind the Trapper's
pack so that it could not be seen. Meanwhile the Trapper pre-

tended to cook flapjacks, and spoke all the time to the elk. 'Come on Prissy,' he said, 'come and have a nice flapjack.' He tossed the rounded slice of bread in the cold pan. The elk remained suspicious.

'I think the tone of your voice is too loud or too deep,' said Chuck. 'Speak softly.'

'I guess it's my accent,' replied the Trapper, 'I'll try him in English. Come on Prissy, old boy, what about a spot of trifle?'

This also had no effect, but presently, with Beryl's coaxing and the sight of his feed bowl hidden behind the pack, Prissy came nearer. When both she and the Trapper had moved away he came right up and picked up the Trapper's blanket, holding it in his mouth. As he pulled the blanket away from the back pack it revealed a bright aluminium suitcase instead of whatever one might expect to find in a trapper's pack. It was quite unsuitable for the film, but Prissy, annoyed either by its brightness or its design, dropped the blanket and attacked it with both fore feet, beating it as a drummer beats his drum.

Order was restored, the pack made up again, and the Trapper knelt on one knee to cook his bread flapjacks again over the cold fire. This time Prissy was no longer nervous. He approached the camp and halted with his lip curled superciliously and a fore leg raised. The Trapper offered him a flapjack and Prissy accepted it. Although he had often watched the moose have their bread, owing to his quick and unpredictable reactions we had never fed him like this. Normally we could never have let him come so close to the Trapper, but his horns were in velvet and he was as gentle as the moose.

The Trapper stroked Prissy's nose and gave him several pieces of bread. 'The Public are never going to believe this,' said Boswell in a hoarse aside. Prissy also found it hard to believe and he soon became overconfident. When the bread ran out he put on his supercilious smile and raised one foot again. There was no more bread. Whereupon the elk put his head down as if he were going to transfix the Trapper and velvet or not, it was time to call a halt. I went up and told him to lay off. Prissy still had a proper respect for me. He gave a shrill whistle and trotted off a few paces then turned to look at us again, head held high, as if to say, 'Look at me – the most beautiful animal in the Canadian woods.' I think that possibly he was right, although Beryl would never agree with me.

The film people came back again and this time Peterkin made an appearance. We had started out to look for him, but hearing our voices he came out of the trees. The sun was low and the aspen trunks looked yellow in its light, their leaves a brilliant green. The moose was chocolate brown below them; his rack, still in velvet, seemed massive but the span was narrower than it would be one day. Still he was an imposing sight and his neck was much bigger than it had been the year before. He advanced slowly, stopping from time to time to study the platoon of strangers in front of him. These now began to waver. Beryl and I wanted the cameramen to be in front so that they could get a picture of his haughty and suspicious approach, but they preferred to have us in front until they knew how he was going to behave.

Chuck got his camera set up and began filming and there were shouts of 'Mind the dog,' and 'can you get the dog back please?' as Dilly ran on ahead unaware that she would ruin the picture. 'Where's the actor?' asked the Director. 'He's coming on as fast as he can but he's crippled in those boots,' answered Vic from the rear.

The Trapper had put on some knee-high laced boots, the sort of things which, from my reading of the 'Wide World' magazine as a boy, I imagined people wore in the Canadian North, where men in just such boots were always fighting off wolves and grizzlies with rifles and hunting knives. He had sat down on a chair on the stone terrace to put them on, grumbling at the Director's instructions, and helped sympathetically by Vic. As Mike had pulled on the boots I noticed that his feet were covered with dabs of mercurochrome where the boots had rubbed him. He came hobbling up with his pack on his back. Peterkin rubbed his horns against a small sapling, put his ears back, rolled his eyes and slobbered. We could not get him to walk after the Trapper as his interest was deflected by the number of people around him. Beryl and I were pretty certain that he would not do anything but he looked impressive as he stalked first after one cameraman then after the other, then after the Trapper, after Boswell who was taking stills and after Vic who was carrying spare film. There were altogether too many people about; Peterkin was confused and a little angry. 'You just have to watch his feet,' explained Beryl. 'He won't use his horns.' In a moment's respite in this game of Tom Tiddler's ground, the Director said to Mike, 'I know it's good acting, but can you manage not to look so nervous.'

'But I am nervous,' said Mike, hobbling away with Peterkin once more stalking after him.

Suddenly there were shouts of 'Here's the other actor,' as Prissy put in an appearance and started to head for the only person who had ever fed him bread. At that moment Beryl said, 'My God there's the cow.' This was much more serious as no one could tell what her reactions would be. Beryl hurried off to meet her and distract her attention with the promise of feed. We began to feel as beleaguered as the British at Isandhlwana and filming for the time being came to an end. Prissy, quick to notice anything to do with food, saw Beryl and Petruska and hurried after them. This meant filming could start again. The picture that they wanted was one of the Trapper walking along by himself followed by a bull moose.

'Go on,' I told him, 'just walk toward the house. Peterkin will follow you.' I knew that Peterkin was just as aware as the elk that there was a distribution of extra rations going on and as soon as Mike moved Peterkin followed him, but to Mike's added alarm walked side by side with him.

Chuck grabbed the hand camera from the Director and ran on in his swift elephant shuffle, making a circuit below them and up to the house so that he could film them as they approached. When Peterkin arrived he found the cow moose still at her feed and moved below the house so that Chuck had a chance of filming him with the lake beyond. 'Give me the tripod, Ford,' he shouted to the Director, but Ford, who had followed behind Peterkin and the actor, had made straight for the house, where Petruska, seeing a stranger close to her, had put her ears back and made a short run towards him, so that he had taken refuge behind a tree and a pile of logs.

'The tripod, the tripod,' called Chuck anxiously.

'Not me,' said Ford, 'I'm not coming out from behind this tree for an Oscar.'

After the cow had been fed she went back to her calves but Peterkin remained with us while Chuck tried to get a shot of the sun setting, framed in Peterkin's horns. The light for filming was soon gone and Peterkin and Prissy decided that their work on the set was over and went down to the pond for a bathe. Chuck could not resist the sight of the two in the water and set off after them at his tireless jog trot, which Boswell told us he could keep up for miles. As he disappeared down the grass road to the pond he reminded me of some great barge coming down the Seine. He was soon back again, still running, mopping his forehead with a huge forearm, but otherwise showing no sign of fatigue. For the time being the career of the moose and the elk as cinema actors was suspended and they turned their attention to getting the velvet off their horns, to war and to sex.

14. Moose Magic
or Madness

On 25 August Beryl walked round the fence in order to mark any holes that might be used by coyotes or porcupines. She had found one or two regular highways under the fence, big enough for Kochi to squeeze under if she so desired although she very rarely left the sanctuary. By now it did not matter if she did, for after the puppies had been weaned we had had her spayed, but we did not want any more dashing blades after Dilly. Poor Chico was unlikely to wander far again, for his owner, exasperated by his wandering habits, had had him castrated. In one way it had been a disastrous mating. Kochi seemed contented and relaxed but just a year after her affair with Chico something, some happy memory, must have stirred her, for Drummond rang me to say that my 'yellow dog' was over looking for Chico.

As Beryl walked round the fence Peterkin appeared, his horns still in velvet. It was exactly a year since he had rubbed the velvet off his last horns. He followed behind her mildly and when she got to the drive stayed behind by the road.

An hour later we left in the car and saw another car drawn up by the fence and against the fence was Peterkin crowned by something tinged with pink and shining. We stopped beside the car and the owner came back from the fence, holding a movie camera. 'I got the whole reel,' he said, 'he's been rubbing the velvet off his horns.' There wasn't a bit of velvet left but only pinkish white bone.

That evening when we fed them on the wall in front of the house, Petruska ran at him as if to strike him, her ears flat down her neck. Peterkin stood his ground for the first time for months. Petruska made the merest gesture of standing up to strike him, but then gave a quavering cry, and wheeled round and came back to the trough. Peterkin stalked haughtily up to feed beside her. Once more and until February, he was lord and master.

From now on we often saw him with her and the calves, sometimes following the calves and checking on them just as a ram checks his ewes, but he was out of luck since they were both bulls. Also they had tangled with porcupines and we had been unable to get near them in order to pull out the quills. Just at the time when they should have been playing together they had been crippled and on the few occasions when we saw them they were both lame. Now one had recovered but the bigger still had a badly swollen fetlock. When Prissy got porcupined he had soon recovered without our help and we had hoped it would be the same with the calves.

Peterkin came into rut again almost as soon as the velvet was off his horns. During the whole of September he was aggressive and attempted to keep Petruska to himself. For several days we saw neither of them. Then there came a time when she tried to get to the house as if seeking help. I saw her once down by the pond and as she attempted to dodge Peterkin he headed her every time until he finally drove her into the water. Next evening she made an even more determined try and this time it appeared that she had the legs of him. He turned like a polo pony to head her while she ran in long zigzags towards the house. On each leg she made a little ground and on her last leg it looked as if she would make it. Peterkin ran like an express train straight for the glass doors. His ears were back and his breath laboured, his flanks heaving. I thought that the wall would never stop him and whether he intended to or not he'd come over the wall and across the terrace into the doors. However he reached the wall just before Petruska and managed to head her. They were both exhausted and the cow waded into the marsh by the house. Peterkin, after blowing like a grampus for a quarter of an hour, allowed his attention to wander and in a moment Petruska was running for the house again. As she ran she gave a whinnying bellow. This time she arrived first but after only a few mouthfuls of feed she went on round behind the owls' enclosure, where she stopped while Peterkin walked slowly after her. Half an hour later she was back again having once more eluded Peterkin. Again she was whinnying as she ran as if the devil himself was after her. The poor devil was, but he followed slowly. Beryl and I had been full of sympathy for Petruska and the way she had been pestered for the last month, but now we began to think that all the running and bellowing were largely for show. When she shook off Peterkin, although she could easily have made good her escape, she hung around until he came up again. We watched the same procedure next day. Again once he had got her away from the house and himself mounted guard, she didn't go off and lose herself in the woods but came back to excite further pursuit. While all this went on the calf that had recovered from its lameness usually appeared but the lame calf stayed away.

On the third evening after this violent pursuit started, we found the whole family group waiting in front of the house. Peterkin was gentle and relaxed and he and Petruska fed together while the calves went down on their knees to eat the clover. It was obvious that something had happened and it was not difficult to guess what. In this peaceful interval I took the opportunity to measure his horns, the first time that he had been quiet enough since he rubbed off the velvet. The spread was exactly fifty inches and each horn had eight points.

Peterkin's rut still wasn't over. He went more often to the fence to see if there were any other moose cows around and he kept a check on Petruska. For three weeks we put Prissy in the drive. He was now two years old and could not leave Petruska alone. Beryl thought that this was too much for her. Prissy was lonely by himself and this year for the first time started bugling, a wild high whistle ending in a grunt. He also made his strange bath tub noises to Beryl and at times was aggressive towards her.

On the day of our first snowfall, a light one soon to disappear, we drove down to the south-east gate where the car, still without winter tyres, stuck on a slight rise. Beryl decided to walk back to bring the Land-Rover. She went round the fence and down the drive, rather than cut across to the house where she might meet Peterkin. In the drive she met Prissy who was so aggressive that she climbed over the drive fence in order to walk down the other side. Meanwhile I had managed to get the car out of the place where it had stuck and when I arrived at the drive gates I saw that Beryl was on the other side of the fence and that Prissy was on the drive side. 'He was making a nuisance of himself,' she shouted to me.

As she said this I noticed that Peterkin was coming up from behind and hurrying towards her. This is going to be an interesting situation, I thought, but as he got up to the fence I saw that it was Prissy he was after. They were soon confronting each other through the fence and Beryl went on her way unmolested.

A few days later she was putting out some feed for Prissy, but concealing her weapon, a broken hoe, against her side, because Peterkin gets angry and upset if he sees her holding the mattock with which she used to chastise him. The hoe was useless for either of them, being far too light. Prissy, thinking that she was unarmed, made a thrust at her. His horns passed each side of her and one roughly brushed her arm. Since then she has taught him greater respect by catching him two whacks on the antlers with the mattock when he has put down his head as if to threaten her. Her aim is to floor him, only if he is insolent, with a good crack on the poll, but he is so quick that it is hard to get home. Like a horse or any other animal, they have to learn proper respect for those who feed them.

The drive gates are fastened by two chains and we both have our own way of fastening them, going in or coming out. When one of us returns we can tell if the other is out or in the sanctuary and if a visitor has been while we were away.

This was the case one evening when Dilly came up to meet us at the gate, to tell us that a stranger had come and to beg a ride back in the truck. There was no note at the house to tell us who had been there but a telephone call that evening identified our visitor.

'Who did you say you are?' I heard Beryl ask doubtfully. 'Kim?' I knew that she was wondering, like me, who Kim might be.

'Chang Kim,' she repeated and then I heard the tone of her voice change to one of delight. 'From China?' Beryl has never forgotten the kindness of the Chinese when she travelled to Chungking and from there to Mitkyina in Burma, by river-boat, by bus, and on her feet, many years ago before the Second World War. By the sound of her voice she might have had a call from Hankow.

'Oh,' she went on, with no noticeable change in enthusiasm, 'from Korea. Of course I should have known. Yes. Come to lunch. Come next Saturday. We should love to see you.'

'Who was that?' I asked her. Beryl has such strange telephone conversations that I would not have been surprised if it had been from a member of the People's Republic.

'It's a Doctor Chang Kim from Calgary. I suppose he's at the University but he's interested in deer. He wants to know if we can keep five deer for him if he gets them. He's interested in their horns. I told him that we had moose and an elk but he didn't seem to think that they would do, or even that they were deer at all.'

'I bet I know what he wants deer's horns for,' I said.

'Well don't you think that we might keep some deer for him, provided that he gets a doe for Prissy? And I'm sure you're wrong. That's rhinoceros horn you're thinking of.'

When Doctor Chang Kim arrived, he came in a large car and turned out to be a Doctor of Physics. He told us that he had been thinking of his retirement and that in Korea horn was in use to cure certain ailments. It was very expensive and you might have to pay up to eight hundred dollars for a treated deer's horn. He said that you couldn't know whether it was the right horn or whether it had been properly prepared. He told us, rather diffidently, that he thought only now were some of the ancient practices of medicine in the East beginning to be appreciated by the West and cited acupuncture as an example. He was gentle, charming and a little shy. Obviously we were not quite what he expected; he had thought that we would go and catch the deer and keep them for him. He had considered starting a small game farm of his own in order to obtain the horn for medicinal purposes, but as he knew nothing about deer, was not a hunter, would have to get a game farm permit and put up a fence before he could even get permission to catch a deer, he had decided to approach us.

'But what sort of deer?' I asked.

'In Korea they are spotted deer.'

'We haven't spotted deer here – it's the Japanese Sika deer

I suppose. But we could let you have moose and elk horn when they shed them.'

'No. That is no good,' said the doctor. 'I think it is small deer that are needed and the horns must be knocked off with a wooden club when they are growing. The animal bleeds but they recover. Then the horn is soft. It is sliced and kept in a cool shady place. When it is required it is boiled and a soup is made to be drunk as medicine. It is full of protein. The horn can be boiled three times, but in Korea you never know how many times it has been boiled before you get it.'

'I suppose whitetail would do?' I suggested.

Dr Kim was disappointed at our lack of enthusiasm. This is the sort of witchcraft, a soup of deer's horn, that Beryl really goes for, but she didn't like the idea of knocking off the horns. We told him that if he gave us a doe for Prissy we would keep his deer for him and would tame them sufficiently so that they could be tranquillized for dehorning, but all the rest was up to him.

Dr Kim seemed doubtful. He looked at us and said. 'It is a very good tonic for people who are over forty and better still for people who are over fifty. I think you will find it of great benefit.'

When he left we asked him if he had a family and would like to bring them out. 'I have four,' he said. 'The eldest fourteen and the youngest – a mistake – only two.'

'Well. There goes your theory,' said Beryl as he left.

'I'm not so sure. You never know when the tree falls,' I replied. 'Someone will ring up and ask us to keep rhinos next.'

September that year was particularly lovely. The golden aspen contrasted brightly with other clumps of trees that had not yet turned, trees of the same species in more sheltered or moister ground. The dark spruce stood like skirmishers before the glory of the autumn reds and yellows. Even the lowly scrub birch was decked in orange, red and brown, while the lake reflected all these colours and the blue skies above. The sun shone but we had had more rain than usual and now that the hay was gone, the fields were green with young clover and alfalfa.

We went down to the pond again and there were the duck that I liked so much; they had nested there and brought up their young, and were now strong on the wing and ready to fly south. Everything seemed to repeat itself, the velvet off Peterkin's horns, the rut, the mating, the falling leaves, almost all on the same day as the year before. Now the duck would soon be gone.

I felt a restlessness for our old freedom and thought how we too, not long ago, might have set sail for the south. In the evening we saw something darker than the surrounding blackness on the slope in front of the house. I switched on the light above the doors. It was Peterkin stretched out on his side and resting his head on his horns like a pillow. 'Is he dead?' asked Beryl anxiously. I slid back the doors. He sat up and turned his head amiably towards us.

We went up to bed, but the restlessness was still with me. 'I don't know what keeps us here,' I said.

'Well, we couldn't have this in England,' Beryl said, knowing how my mind wanders. 'All this space, and the animals, and so much to do.'

I looked out of the window again. Peterkin was still chewing the cud below and from somewhere beyond the fence came the lilting call of a coyote. Kochi was barking in reply. It must be the moose holding us, I thought. A kind a madness. A kind of magic. Moose Magic?